# SHARED COURAGE

# SHARED COURAGE

## A Marine Wife's Story
## of Strength and Service

MICHELLE KEENER

ZENITH PRESS

*This book is dedicated to the wives and families of the Marines and sailors who served with 3rd Battalion, 4th Marines, during Operation Iraqi Freedom. May your sacrifices never be forgotten.*

*And to my husband, who came home safely.*

First published in 2007 by Zenith Press, an imprint of MBI Publishing Company, Galtier Plaza, Suite 200, 380 Jackson Street, St. Paul, MN 55101-3885 USA

Zenith Press titles are also available at discounts in bulk quantity for industrial or sales-promotional use. For details write to Special Sales Manager at MBI Publishing Company, Galtier Plaza, Suite 200, 380 Jackson Street, St. Paul, MN 55101-3885 USA.

To find out more about our books, join us online at www.zenithpress.com.

Library of Congress Cataloging-in-Publication Data

Keener, Michelle, 1973-
  Shared courage : a fighting-Marine wife's story / Michelle Keener.
    p. cm.
  ISBN-13: 978-0-7603-2996-2 (hardbound)
  ISBN-10: 0-7603-2996-6 (hardbound)
  1. Iraq War, 2003-   2. Keener, Michelle, 1973-   3. Marine Corps spouses--United States--Biography.   I. Title.
DS79.76.K45 2007
956.7044'3--dc22

                                            2006025151

**Front cover photo:** The author and her husband Paul at a formal dinner event in April 2005, celebrating the return of the 7th Marine Regiment to Twentynine Palms, California. *Photo by Julie Walton*

Editor: Steve Gansen
Designer: Brenda C. Canales
Jacket Design: Melissa K. Khaira

Printed in the United States of America

# CONTENTS

# FOREWORD

The military saying, "those who wait also serve," is absolutely true, but incomplete in times of war. To be complete, one must add in several words. The first is *suffer*. Those who wait suffer through hundreds of sleepless nights, endure the sudden sinking of hope and the rise of fear with each announcement of adverse events or casualties on the news or through the military's expanded grapevine. They suffer the purgatory of putting every dream, every hope, every shared plan for the future on hold, and at times live minute by minute, fearing it might all end with that dreaded knock at the door. Military families today also suffer through living in a society largely oblivious to such sacrifices, unsympathetic to their plight since it is in effect a choice, and at times dismissive of the concept of service. The word *suffer* itself does not complete the saying. The final word is *love*.

Having served through three combat tours, with two as the commanding officer of 3rd Battalion, 4th Marines where Michelle's husband Paul also served, I have seen many acts of courage. Physical courage on the battlefield is a noble and just thing. But the most inspiring display of courage is that special courage inspired by love. That is the courage displayed by those who wait and experience war secondhand in action, but first-hand in emotion and shared sacrifice. This is the story told here.

Nearly twenty-five hundred years ago, the battle for the West was fought. Western civilization, the very concept of Western democracy, was under assault from the Persia. The Persian King Xerxes with a two million-man army marched on Greece with the intent to enslave its citizens, as he had the rest of the known world. As the Greek city states debated how to deal with the approaching juggernaut, to fight, to appease, or to have each state sue for its own separate peace, the Spartans marched. King Leonidas led three hundred hand-picked Spartans to Thermopylae, a narrow pass between the mountains and sea, and faced down the invading army. Against all odds the Spartans and their allies held off the Persians for seven days. Finally, their weapons broken and bodies weakened by wounds and exhaustion, they died fighting to the last man. Their sacrifice galvanized the fractured and frightened Greek cities and provided the inspiration that rallied the Greeks to final victory a year later at Plataea and saved Western democracy in its infancy.

The three hundred hand picked Spartans stood at the pass and saved the West while their countrymen debated and bickered. Leonidas chose these men not for their talent as warriors. Not all were champion athletes, and none were expendable. They were chosen for the courage of their women. Women possessed of character who "would drink the cup of poison" and bear with stoic dignity the loss of their sons and husbands and provide the example of poise. They would be the rock that the rest of Greece would stand upon. Today, the West and its democracy are under assault from terrorists that despise our freedoms, and there are but a precious few in the West willing to stand in the pass and stem the tide of aggression. The enemy is watching us and waiting for our lines to crack, not on the field of battle, but at home. In this kind of war, the real battlefield is the hearts and minds of the home front, and it is fought by ladies like Michelle, Krista, Stephanie, Jennifer, Ann, Jo, and countless anonymous others that each day shoulder the burden of service, suffering, and love, send their men to war, and wait. In doing so they share their courage with each other and are the rock the rest of America stands upon during these uncertain times.

Michelle has created a must-read work. This book is a must for anyone preparing to send a loved one to war, and a must for any commander leading Americans in harm's way. On a certain level I understood the struggle our families faced during our deployments, but I did not truly fathom the depth of emotion, the roller coaster ride of euphoric highs and gut-wrenching lows that punctuate a deployment. I did not understand the daily battles fought by the unsung heroes of the home front. Battles fought against not just despair, fear, and uncertainty but also against the unwitting allies of these dreads, the uncaring bureaucrat, the clueless reporter looking for a headline, and the oblivious citizen that makes an ignorant and insensitive comment that exacerbates the pressures of separation.

Michelle and those like her not only bore these burdens themselves but chose to volunteer to lead and provide support for others through their example of poise and unfailing advice. The reader will be treated to a story full of suspense, humor, despair, and euphoria and will walk away with a first hand account of the war waged at home in our neighborhoods, shopping centers, little league gatherings and day care centers. The fact that this war passes practically unnoticed is a tribute to their pride and stoicism and grace. This is their story.

—*Col. Bryan McCoy*
*3rd Battalion, 4th Marine Regiment*

# ACKNOWLEDGMENTS

This book would not have been possible without the help and support of so many people. I am indebted to all of the wives of 3rd Battalion, 4th Marines (Three-Four) who went through Operation Iraqi Freedom with me. This book comes from the strength and courage you all showed during that difficult time. I will always be proud to have been a part of that group, and I thank each of you for inspiring me. Krista Boyce, my friend, who first encouraged me to do this. You are one of the strongest women I have ever met. Julie Walton, who has never let me falter on this journey and who keeps me laughing. Jennifer Johnston, who brought so much strength to our group of friends in Twentynine Palms. The Key Volunteers, who gave so much of themselves to help others: Ann Baker, Monica Coughlin, Stephanie Dillbeck, Aime Fountain, Heather Green, Rebecca Hammond, Kristy Hayes, Alli Jimenez, Monica Langella, Venus Martinez-Robinson, Krissy Moreno, Erika Norton, Kelly Pagliei, Brandy Parkin, Lynde Phillips, Mary Pittman, Stacy Pleger, Rebecca Reyes, Ingrid Rockman, Jo Rosbough, Misty Thompson, and Jessica Wessman. Your dedication and commitment still amazes me.

I must also thank the men who made this book possible: John Koopman for his guidance in the book world and his invaluable advice and kindness; Colonel Bryan McCoy, my most ardent supporter on this project, whose encouragement, words of wisdom, and honest editorial advice have been the backbone of this book and to whom I am deeply humbled by all of your support; Major Andy Petrucci, who kept me sane during the second deployment and who is still my favorite guy to harass.

Special thanks to Richard Kane and Steve Gansen at Zenith Press for all of their help in guiding me through the writing and publishing process.

Finally, I wish to thank my parents, who gave so much of their time and love to me during the deployments. Thank you for knowing when I needed help and couldn't ask for it. Thank you for coming to visit me just when the pressure was getting to be too much. And thank you for always encouraging me to follow my love of writing.

To my daughter, Emily, who was my biggest reason for getting up every day during the deployments. You are the joy and light of my life.

To my son, Brett, who has given our family a new measure of happiness. May this book inspire you to grow up to be just like your father.

And to my husband, Paul. You are the true reason this book exists, because without you I wouldn't belong to this wonderful, strange military world. I would go through any war if you were by my side. You are my best friend, and I love you.

With deepest gratitude,
*Michelle*

# INTRODUCTION

I've noticed that you generally only see military wives in the media two times: once when their husbands are going off to war, and once when their husbands are returning from war. No one ever really knows what goes on in between those two events. Do the wives just curl up and hibernate until their men return home? Well, after being married to a Marine for six years and having gone through two combat deployments with him, I can safely say: no, we don't hibernate.

My husband, Paul, and I had been married for just over two years when he was sent to Iraq for the first time. He left me with a seven-month-old daughter in the middle of the California desert, where it was thirty minutes to the nearest Wal-Mart (over an hour to Target). Contrary to the news coverage, my life didn't stop when my husband went to war. I still had a daughter to care for and bills to pay. I also had an incredible circle of friends who were going through the same thing I was going through. We were a small community of Marine Corps wives, and we all had to find a way to get through the war. Our husbands served and fought together, they mourned together, and most of them came home together. What has so often been overlooked though, even by ourselves, is that when our husbands went to war, we served too.

It has been two years since Paul returned from his last deployment, and it has taken me that long to realize that I went to war too. I may not have had an M-16 in my hands (though there were days I sorely wanted one), and I didn't have to live on military food or sleep in a small tent, but it was still war. The war was in my living room, on my TV as I watched Fox News nonstop for days at a time. It was in the grocery store when I stocked up on nonperishable food to send in care packages to Paul. The war was at my front door whenever the doorbell rang unexpectedly and my heart stopped beating for a moment as I prayed there weren't Marines in dress blues waiting on the other side to tell me that Paul was never coming home. The war was there when I'd visit with other Marine wives and all we could talk about was who had heard from her husband and did anyone know where the battalion was headed. The war was in my home when my baby girl would look at a picture of her father and not know who he was. No, I may not have been to Iraq, but I've been to war.

I married a Marine Corps officer knowing full well that there was a chance that someday he would go to war. But that someday always seemed so far away. When Paul was commissioned, I stood by his side, and I had never been so proud in my life. He was standing in his dress-blue uniform looking so handsome and serious and all I could do was smile. Then less than three years later, the day that seemed so far away arrived. When Paul left for Iraq, I stood by his side once again and cried. But then my work really started. My life didn't end when my husband went to war, but it was never the same again.

This book is the story of my life during those two deployments. Not long after our husbands returned from Iraq, my friend Krista and I went out to dinner. Over dessert we were reminiscing about everything that happened during the war. I jokingly said that I should write a book about it someday, and Krista agreed. Not because my life was the most interesting or the most exciting, but because we both recognized that the wives left behind during the war had a story to tell, too. And just like the war our husbands fought in the deserts and towns of Iraq, it isn't always pretty. It isn't a story that comes with a guaranteed happy ending, because none of us ever knew what tomorrow would bring. The wives of the Marines in the 3rd Battalion, 4th Marines who went through Operation Iraqi Freedom had to endure stress and worry and fear that we could never have imagined possible before the war. There are stories of great courage and great sadness. They are the stories of the women who waited and prayed and hoped, the women who wrote letters and sent care packages and showed their children pictures of their fathers every day so they wouldn't be forgotten. This is the other side of war.

In the poem "On His Blindness," John Milton wrote, "They also serve who only stand and wait." This book is my story, but I hope that it gives a voice to all of the other military wives who went through the Iraq War—and, those who are still going through it. Maybe no one notices what we do, maybe we don't get medals for it, but what we do matters. Our courage doesn't exist on a distant battlefield, but in the every day acts that keep our families together. We also serve.

# Chapter 1

# WELCOME TO THE MARINE CORPS

I was going to be a nun. It sounds ridiculous now, but when I met my future husband, I was looking into religious orders, deciding which habits brought out the color of my eyes, which convent got the least amount of snow. I can joke about it now, but in 1999 I was very serious. I was living in San Diego, having moved there four years earlier to attend law school. As it turned out, I loved San Diego and hated law school. After a dismal year and a half, I left law to pursue my master's degree in theology. Meanwhile, the man I would someday marry was working as a bouncer in a bar that my friend Juliana and I would frequent on Friday nights. She and I lived in neighboring apartment complexes, and the bar was right down the hill—good for walking home after a night of girl talk and amaretto sours.

Paul and I hit it off right away, but stayed "just friends" for months. I had recently ended a four-year relationship; my ex was a bodybuilder who decided he wanted to be a priest (keep reading, my life is never boring). I had no intention of getting involved with anyone ever again— nun, remember? But Paul was funny and smart and sweet. He would always stop by our table at the bar and check up on us. More than once he chased away guys who had trouble taking no for an answer. We shared stories over drinks and got to know each other in that flirty, but not-really-going-to-go-anywhere way. He told me he was working his way through college and majoring in political science. He'd enlisted in the U.S. Army at seventeen and had been stationed all over the world. After the army he had done a variety of jobs, including working as a fisherman in Alaska, a chef in Florida, an engineer in the merchant marines, and a welder in the naval reserves. Now he was finishing his degree and applying for a commission in the Marine Corps. Well, that was a lot of information to take in, and since I had no intention of dating him, I didn't worry too much at the mention of the Marine Corps. I was more concerned about the fact that he had a unibrow.

One night I was feeling particularly down in the dumps. I can't remember why now, but I was twenty-five, I had a brand-new master's degree but no job, and I was single and in a bar—not a good combination. Paul noticed that I seemed sad and tried to cheer me up. He finally asked me to go out for coffee the next week. I smiled and very politely declined.

"Thanks, that's really nice, but I don't think so." (He has a unibrow! And I'm going to be a nun, right?)

"It would be fun. We can go out just as friends, that's all. You're too beautiful to be so sad."

*Ok*, I think, *that's not going to work on me.* No compliment given in bar can ever be taken seriously.

"I'm really not up for it. I hate men."

"Good," he grinned. "So do I."

And that was it. He had me at "So do I." I finally agreed to go—just as friends. He picked me up three days later and the rest is history. We spent every free minute together. He proposed on my birthday two months later. Eventually we found out that both of us knew on our third date that we were going to get married. It was that kind of instant clarity where you suddenly saw the next fifty years of your life in someone else's eyes. Wonderful— and terrifying. Paul never doubted our future for a second; I freaked out repeatedly over the next year leading up to our wedding.

Two weeks after our engagement, Paul left for officer candidate school. I still wasn't too worried about the fact that my future husband was going to be a Marine officer. I mean, it's just a job, right? How bad could it be? (Pause here for all military wives reading this to laugh knowingly.)

I felt pretty well prepared, actually. Both of my grandfathers had been in the military. One was a Navy warrant officer whose ship had been stationed at Pearl Harbor and was fortunately out to sea the day of the attack. My maternal grandfather, my papa, had been a career Air Force officer. He was a rocket scientist—seriously, an actual rocket scientist. He was the smartest man I've ever met, and he kept a buzz cut until the day he died. I looked at my mom and figured she turned out pretty well for a military brat. My father, whom I love and adore, had been drafted into the army during the Vietnam War. During boot camp, he had actually volunteered to go to medic school. He was either being incredibly brave or incredibly stupid. (He's the first one to say stupid. I'll stick with brave.) He did become a medic, but was stationed in Puerto Rico his entire tour. Talk about lucky. I figured with my family background I would slip right into military life.

It was six months after Paul and I got married that I had my first taste of what lay ahead. In the Marine Corps, all newly commissioned officers must attend a six-month course called the Basic School. This requirement has to do with the Marine Corps philosophy that "every Marine is a rifleman." The Basic School, or TBS (everything in the military can be reduced to an acronym), teaches every officer how to lead an infantry platoon. It also covers basic leadership skills, marksmanship, and the nuts and bolts of how to be an officer. Most importantly, it is also the time when officers are told what military occupational specialty (MOS) they will be assigned—for example, supply, infantry, intelligence, or logistics. This is a huge deal. Your MOS is essentially your job within the Marine Corps. In other branches of service, you can select your MOS when you sign up, so you know what you're getting into when you sign your name on the dotted line. Not so with the Marine Corps. Marines don't find out what their "job" will be until it's too late to back out. It sounds frightening, but it encourages the idea that every Marine is a Marine first and a radio operator, intel officer, or military policeman second.

Paul and I were married in May, and Paul was sched-uled to go to TBS in Virginia in November. We talked for a long time about whether or not I would go with him to Virginia or remain in California. It may seem like a pretty easy decision. I was home working on my first novel at the time, so I didn't have a job conflict and we were still newlyweds. So I should go, right? On the other hand, Paul explained that because of the TBS schedule, he wouldn't be home all the time; he would be out in the field (a generic term for the times when Marines disappear for days or weeks at a time to go do training exercises in some remote location and come home dirty, smelly, and tired) quite a bit, and he wouldn't have much time to spend with me. We also didn't know what his MOS was going to be, so we didn't know where we would be living once TBS ended. If he were selected for artillery, he would have to go to Fort Sill, Kentucky, for training. If he were given infantry he would stay at Quantico, Virginia, for his additional schooling. Once his MOS training was complete he would then move to his first duty station. So we were looking at possibly three moves in one year, and all of it was up in the air. After much discussion we decided that I would stay in California with my mom and he would go to TBS alone. So after only six months of marriage we encountered our first military separation. (I always try to clarify our separations as strictly geographic when talking to people outside of the military. If I just say "yeah, we've been separated three times," people start handing out their therapists' business cards.)

All in all, that first seperation wasn't too bad. Paul came home only a month later for Christmas leave. I was able to fly out to Virginia twice to visit him, and we spent our first wedding anniversary together in Washington, D.C. But in what would eventually become a tradition, we were apart for my birthday. About halfway through TBS Paul called and said we had to discuss his MOS request list. He had to list all thirty of the possible MOS assignments in order of preference. Paul's theory was that the first five were most important because he was at the top of his class, and he thought he had a pretty good chance of getting one of his top choices.

There were many long phone calls, many e-mails fired back and forth over the course of a week or so. Paul wanted my input and my approval on his choices. I was afraid of making that decision for him (oh, the bliss of newlywed life, when you didn't want to push your opinions on your spouse). I kept telling him it was his career and he had to do what would make him happy. In this case Paul had far more insight than I did and explained that this was going to affect our family for years to come. It was a big decision, and I started to find myself totally out of my element. After many long nights we finally came up with his top five:

1. Communications (computers, radios, and gadgets)
2. Logistics (not the guy who planned D-day, but the guy who figured out how many boats they needed)
3. Signals Intelligence (listening to bad guys talk on phones and radios)
4. Tanks (driving an armored tank over smaller objects with no fear of getting a ticket)
5. Artillery (blowing stuff up from far away)

Getting something paperwork-related was Paul's worst fear. After he submitted his list of preferences we had to wait another two months or so until he found out what he would be doing.

Communications—he got his first choice, and we were both thrilled. (I think deep down Paul was probably secretly hoping for something that involved blowing up stuff or running over things, but he never mentioned it.) He was in communications during his enlistment with the army, so he felt pretty comfortable with what he would be doing. The Computer Information Systems Officer Course, where Paul would go through his MOS training, was also located in Quantico. It was a nine-month course, so we decided that I would move out there as soon as TBS finished.

In June 2001, Paul graduated from TBS and flew back to California on graduation day. We packed up the little we hadn't already put in storage, loaded it into my car, and off we went to Virginia. It felt like an adventure. I had never lived outside of California. I was born near Los Angeles, and my family moved to northern California when I was four. By the time I went to high school I was itching to move back to L.A. At eighteen I went to college in a small town north of L.A., and after graduation I moved to San Diego. I was a California girl through and through. Even now Paul teases me about the L.A. accent that occasionally pops out my mouth. There aren't many of us who can still use words like "whatever," "dude," and "awesome" with a straight face.

I loved the trip across the country. Paul and I had a wonderful time. We still enjoy road trips together and have no problem spending hours a day in the small confines of a car. The only rules are that Paul always drives and I work the invisible door-handle brake. We took the southern route and passed through Amarillo, Texas, and the Air Force base where my mother was born. During the trip to

Virginia we drove through a southern state that shall remain nameless because it was such a travel nightmare. There was only one highway that went through the state, and the entire road was under construction. Not just a segment here or there, but the whole thing. That was a new level of frustration in my life, and I vowed never to cross that state again.

When we made it to Tennessee we had to find a detour through a backwoods area to avoid a traffic accident. While filling up in Watertown (population maybe twenty) we met a nice man who goggled over our California license plates. He asked us what I have come to label the standard California questions: Did you know any celebrities? And do you know how to surf? He was only mildly disappointed when we said no to both. A few days later when we stopped for dinner, the waiter politely asked where we were from. When I said California he held his hand to his heart and asked if I was one of those "tofu-eatin' space cadets." OK, I may be a vegetarian who has been known to push tiny pieces of tofu on my husband, but I'm no space cadet.

When we finally made it to Quantico, Paul began talking up the base house we had been given. He had checked it out before he left and had already moved in the stuff he had with him at TBS. The house was great, he assured me. It was a townhouse style with a big backyard and a covered patio. It was two stories, three bedrooms, and had all hardwood floors except for tile in the kitchen. I was beyond excited about our first real house. I had

Donna Reed fantasies about cooking gourmet dinners in our beautiful kitchen then snuggling up to watch TV in our fabulously decorated living room. I imagined us planting flowers in the front yard and having a wrought-iron patio set in the back. I think I was channeling *Better Homes and Gardens* by the time we reached the base.

Marine Corps Base Quantico is an imposing sight. There is a small version of the Iwo Jima flag-raising statue outside the main gate and a huge sign over the road announcing "Quantico, Crossroads of the Marine Corps." We slowed down at the gate and waited for the guard to wave us through. He glanced at the blue sticker on the car windshield, then snapped a salute and waved us through. I asked Paul why he saluted when Paul wasn't in uniform.

"It's the sticker. Red stickers are for enlisted personnel. Blue stickers are for officers and whenever you recognize an officer, you salute."

"Oh."

"They'll salute you, too, when you drive through the gate."

"Me?" I stammered. "Why? I'm not in the Marines."

"But you've got the sticker on your car."

"What am I supposed to do?" I was suddenly feeling again like a fish out of water. I didn't want Marines saluting me. It didn't feel right. "Do I tell them I'm not a Marine or do I salute back?"

Paul turned his head and grinned at me. "Just smile and wave."

"Oh," I said. "I can do that."

We drove up the long, winding road from the front gate to Mainside. Mainside is the part of a base where most things are centered—the commissary, the exchange, administrative offices, the military police, that sort of thing. Quantico is beautiful. Huge trees line the road, everything is green, the buildings are done in colonial brick facades, and there's the Medal of Honor golf course where Paul played during TBS and quickly became addicted. Only a few blocks into Mainside we turned right and headed past the stadium. Going up the hill we entered part of the housing area. My Donna Reed fantasy started to crumble, bit by bit.

The first houses we passed were small, worn down, and dingy. That's not a word that applies to much, but *dingy* definitely worked here.

"Is this where we live?" I could feel my throat closing up as we drove higher up the hill.

"No," Paul said easily. "This is enlisted housing. Officer country is farther up."

"Oh, OK." I exhaled a truly selfish sigh of relief. We drove farther up, passing the base elementary school. "Look, they have a school."

"This base has just about everything. It's a separate world."

Just past the school there was a large break in the houses. We made a turn and stumbled upon six huge buildings. All brick facades, shuttered windows, beautiful lawns. *Oh please, let us live here.*

"Is this it?" I ask again. *Please, please, please.*

"Nope." (*Crap.*) "These are the lettered apartments.

Mostly field grade in here." Field-grade officers are majors, lieutenant colonels, and colonels. Paul was a second lieutenant at the time, the very bottom of the company-grade officers.

"So where do we live?" I finally asked. *How much farther could this road go on?*

"We're almost there, it's just around the corner."

We drove around the apartment buildings, past a pair of very old tennis courts, and entered another housing area. My heart stopped. The houses were the same as the ones we passed on the way up. The dingy ones. We turned at the first left and drove to the end of a, well, a dead-end street. It couldn't really have been called a cul-de-sac. The road just stopped at a row of houses. The official name for our housing area was 300-block housing. But Marines and families who have lived in this area refer to it in such glowing terms as "the crack houses" or "the lieu-tena-ments." The entire area has since been scheduled to be torn down and replaced with brand new housing. Of course, that happened four years after we moved out.

"This is it," Paul said as he parked the car. I couldn't breathe and just stared at the ugliest set of townhouses I had ever seen. We were at the very end of the street. If a car lost its brakes and just kept going down the road, they'd have ended up in our living room. "Let's go." Paul opened the door for me and had the nerve to look happy to be home.

There was a large lawn that extended in front of all four homes in our little set and then over to both groups of neighboring houses. The bottom half of the house was done in brick and the top in white paneling. Outside there was a strange brick wall that jutted out for seemingly no reason. As I peeked around I saw it hid our trash can and our leaking air conditioner. We followed the cracked, gray sidewalk up to the front door. Next to the front door was another door that Paul said led to the laundry room and storage shed. As he opened the squeaky screen and unlocked the front door, I took a deep breath and figured it couldn't get much worse.

I hate being wrong. All Donna Reed images fled in terror as I stepped inside. There were indeed hardwood floors—the original flooring installed when the houses were built seventy years ago. We went downstairs to the living room and kitchen area. Dead bug carcasses littered the floor. "Guess they sprayed," Paul offered. My numb silence must have worried him because he finally started to look nervous.

I wandered into the kitchen and had to bite my lip. The tile floor Paul raved about was in fact linoleum cut into tile shapes and also seventy years old. The kitchen was tiny. It had no dishwasher, no garbage disposal, and one window that looked out onto our leaky air conditioner.

Upstairs wasn't much better. We had one bathroom with blue tile walls and stained linoleum floors. There were two proper bedrooms and one something-else room. This was the "sunroom" as the housing worker who came by to do our initial inspection later informed us. This was the same lady who told us not to eat the paint chips because there was lead paint on the walls. ("Oh, don't worry," she assured us, "We've covered it over with five layers of lead-free paint.") The sunroom had a bare concrete floor, brick walls, and exposed pipes. Of course it did have two big windows—I guess that's where the "sun" part came from.

When I came back downstairs, Paul looked up at me hopefully. "So, what do you think?"

I immediately burst into tears.

# Chapter 2

# QUANTICO

We need curtains. When I finally stopped crying, that was the first thing I said. We unloaded the car and immediately drove to the nearest Wal-Mart. Paul must have felt terrible about my disappointment because he didn't object to anything in the growing pile of decorations that I decided we needed. We left with cream curtains and burgundy scarves, matching area rugs (lots of them), a new shower curtain, bath mats, and a bunch of other items I deemed absolutely necessary.

I actually felt much better the next day when we had covered the mismatched roller blinds with the new curtains and the stained floors with the rugs. We were sleeping on an air mattress at the time because our household goods wouldn't be delivered for another two weeks. Summer is always the busiest time for the military movers, and we were pretty far down the list for deliveries. So we had to be content with eating off paper plates and watching TV on Paul's computer monitor, which fortunately had a cable connection. It actually wasn't a bad time—kind of like camping, except that we had indoor plumbing.

On the day we moved in we met our first neighbors, Brian and Cathy Russell. They lived in the end unit of our group of townhouses. Brian was a captain, and he was attending the Advanced Warfighting School (AWS), also known as "Captain School." Cathy was pregnant and due in January. They also had two huge Labradors, Boomer and Shadow. We went over to borrow their phone so we could call to arrange to have ours hooked up. Brian mentioned that he had a friend moving into the unit between ours within the next week or so, another captain attending AWS. When we went back home, Paul frowned and said "I hope they're not all captains."

Sure enough they were. All three of our neighbors were captains attending AWS. Steve and Justine Pritchard were the friends Brian said were moving in. Brian and Steve had been stationed together in Camp Lejeune as lieutenants, and they were both in artillery. Brad and Lara Bean moved into the other end unit, the one right next to us; Brad was in intelligence. And all three of the wives were pregnant and due within a month of each other.

It turned out to be a great group of people. We all got together once a month for dinner, and we rotated who would host it. We were all on a first-name basis, and Brian, Steve, and Paul became drinking buddies. Paul was nervous at first, being a second lieutenant surrounded by captains. With military etiquette rules, the fact that our new neighbors all outranked Paul could have made life at home for him very awkward. But no one insisted on being called "Sir," and no one pressured Paul to mow the huge lawn every week or otherwise tried to take advantage of his lower rank. Of course my husband, stickler for military protocol that he is, probably would have done it.

As for the wives, we all started walking together. The expectant moms, all having their first child, wanted some exercise, and I wanted company. None of us were working, so we saw quite a bit of each other. Paul and I were trying to get pregnant as well, so I was getting plenty of free advice as to how to make it happen. We'd walk the trails in the woods behind our houses and talk about everything. I also gained a lot of insight into how the military wife society worked.

As much as I enjoyed our neighbors and was getting used to our house, I was still nervous about living on base. I got butterflies whenever I went into the commissary (our version of a grocery store) or the exchange (a department store). In order to shop at these stores you have to show your military identification card. Even though I had mine and I knew it was OK, it still took me a while to get used to it. And driving through the gate the first time just about sent me into a nervous breakdown. What if they didn't let me back in? What would I do? Again, silly fears now, but four years ago they were all very real. The first time the guard waved me through and saluted the sticker (not me, the sticker) I did just what Paul said, smiled and waved. The guard didn't smile back, but he let me through.

By September, we had fallen into a good routine. Paul was in communications school and loving every minute of it. He's a born computer geek—who also happens to know how to assemble and fire a variety of deadly weapons. I was working out at the gym on base (you think Twenty-Four Hour Fitness is intimidating? Try working out with a bunch of Marines!). And I was reading everything I could find on how to get pregnant. I hadn't gotten used to not working, but I was finding plenty of ways to keep myself busy.

One morning, I had decided to skip the gym, and I was puttering around the house when Paul called.

"Have you seen the news?"

"No, I haven't turned on the TV yet. Why?"

"Someone just crashed a plane into the World Trade Center."

"You're kidding."

"No, I'm not. Where's your mom?" My mom is a flight attendant for United Airlines.

"I think she's still in London." *Was she still in London? When was she supposed to fly home?* I couldn't remember— she told me, but I wasn't paying very close attention.

"Go turn on the news and try to stay off the phone. The base is going on alert, and they'll need the phone lines. I'll be home as soon as I can."

I ran downstairs and turned on the TV. It was September 11, 2001. There were news bulletins breaking into all programming to report the plane crash, but it was still so calm. We were all still thinking, hoping, that it had been a terrible accident. I was watching when the second plane crashed, then when they reported that there was a fire at the Pentagon and a plane crashing in Pennsylvania. I remember thinking, *Planes are falling from the sky. How many more are there?* I was watching when the towers fell.

I'm sure it's one of those days that we will all remember forever, and we will all remember exactly where we were when it happened. It will eventually become a question our children ask out of curiosity: "Where were you on September 11?" The way I asked my parents where they were when Kennedy was shot or when

Elvis died.

I worried about my mom. It was hours later when I received a call from the mother of the flight attendant with whom my mom was staying in London. They had been trying to call since the first reports, but the phones lines were all tied up. The mother who called, Mrs. Pender, said her son had asked her to call me and let me know my mom was fine, but that she was still in London and didn't know when she would be able to get back. All flights had been grounded.

I was also worried about Paul's uncle who worked occasionally at the Pentagon. But Paul got through to him and found out he was safe as well. I called my dad shortly after the news broke about the Pentagon. Quantico is only thirty minutes or so south from the Pentagon, and I knew he'd be worrying. (In college I had been close to the center of the Northridge quake, and my parents had been worried sick when they couldn't get through to me right away.) When my dad answered, I told him quickly that we were fine and that Paul was on his way home. Then I stayed off the phone.

I don't think I left the house at all that day. When Paul came home he told me the base had been locked down. No one was getting on or off. He had offered our guest room and our couch to some Marines who lived off base and didn't know if they'd be able to get home that night.

The next day when Paul left for school we were both in a kind of daze.

"If you leave the house," he told me "make sure you

take your ID card with you. They're checking everyone. And don't go off base, they may lock it down again."

Cathy came over, and we went for a walk in the woods. A normal part of our day, but it suddenly felt so abnormal. We both had our ID cards in our pockets, and we were both silent. There just didn't seem to be anything to say. Eventually, we cut it short and just went home.

When I went to the exchange later that day, just to get out of the house, I couldn't believe my eyes.

Quantico had armed Marines patrolling the streets. Not just policemen walking around—I mean Marines with flak jackets, helmets, and loaded M-16s walking the streets. I never made it to the exchange. I went home and watched the news instead.

The base remained on alert. A number of times they locked it down for a few hours in response to terrorist threats. Gone were the days of driving up to the gate and just being waved through. Everyone was stopped. ID cards were scrutinized carefully; bomb-sniffing dogs and Marines with mirrors checked cars for explosives. They instituted random car searches. Paul and I were stopped once coming through the back gate. We were asked to pull over and get out. Our IDs were checked and our car was searched inside and out. Good thing I hadn't done any lingerie shopping that day.

And it wasn't just getting on and off base that changed. Doors to the buildings on base were locked. You had to flash your ID card through the glass before they would unlock the doors. Workers were stationed at the commissary and exchange entrances and checked your ID before you even went in. All nonmilitary events were cancelled. Even the soccer practices for the base youth program, which Paul and I had been coaching, were cancelled for a while.

It was such a surreal time to be living on the base. Half the time we couldn't figure out if we were safer on base or more of a target. Eventually, though, we got used to it. It's amazing what your mind can adapt to. The sight of M-16s on my way down the road stopped being a shock, and I was always ready with my ID card. We saw on the news the outpouring of patriotism in communities around the country: all the flags and banners and parades. The funny thing is, that didn't really happen on base. There wasn't an explosion of red, white, and blue.

Later it occurred to me what was really going on.

We were all waiting.

When troops started going into Afghanistan, it finally hit home. We were all waiting to see who would be going next. In our neighborhood almost every one of the Marines was in school. Where would they go when school finished? Who was going to go to Afghanistan, and as time wore on, would anyone go to Iraq? We didn't need the red-white-and-blue displays to show our patriotism—we had green. Green camouflage uniforms and the certainty that someone was going to war. It was just a matter of time.

Right after September 11, like thousands of other people around the country, I thought about joining the military. Paul supported the idea and tried to talk me into the Marines, but I was leaning to the Air Force because of my grandfather. I had contacted a recruiter online and was talking to Paul about the details of joining when I got some suprising news.

When Paul came home from school, I sat down on the couch next to him.

"Guess what?" I prompted him.

"What?" He replied, not really listening.

"I think I'm pregnant."

"Oh, good." Then he picked up the remote control and turned on the TV. I sat in shock and just stared at him for a full minute. Then he sat up, turned the TV off, and looked at me. "What did you say?"

"I'm pregnant."

Then I got the reaction I had been waiting for. He gave me a huge hug and started asking all the questions I didn't have answers to. When was the baby due? How pregnant was I?

We agreed not to tell anyone until we made it through the first trimester. I'm a good Irish girl and thus as super-stitious as can be. Of course that didn't stop Paul from telling Brian and Steve one night while they were hanging out after one of our dinner parties. When Paul confessed that he had spilled the beans, he swore that both men had promised not to tell their wives. Both wives knew later that same night. When I finally made my announcement a few weeks later, it wasn't much of a surprise anymore.

The year 2001 rolled into 2002. All three of our neigh-bors had healthy babies and disappeared into their own newborn baby's world. I was thrilled to be pregnant, but frustrated that I couldn't do any decorating for our new baby. Paul's school ended in May, and we would be moving eight weeks before the baby was due. So there wasn't much point in setting up a nursery that would just be packed up and moved. Of course I still managed to do quite a bit of shopping for the little one.

As communications school drew to an end, Paul had to submit his list of preferences for his first duty station. We talked about it for a long time and decided that we wanted to go to Twentynine Palms. Now, Twentynine Palms is usually considered a rotten place to be sent. It's in the middle of the California desert surrounded by nothing. Nothing but sand and dry brush as far as the eye can see. However, we were expecting our first child, and my mom was living in Palm Springs, only an hour away from Twentynine Palms. The rest of our family lives in California, as well, so Twentynine Palms seemed like the perfect place for us. Not surprisingly there aren't many people who voluntarily request to go to Twentynine Palms, so Paul got his first choice pretty easily.

As for me, I needed something more to do than just debate baby names so I decided to go through Key Volunteer Network training. The Key Volunteer Network (KVN) is an organization of volunteer spouses who provide information and resources for military families. The KVN acts as a communication liaison between the green side (the Marines and the command of each unit) and the families. If this sounds like a practiced speech that's because it is; I've given it many times. What we really do is pass along important information to the families in our unit and provide answers to their questions about base and military resources. Families can call us whenever they need to ask questions or if they're having a problem, and we try to help them find the right resource to solve it—military or civilian. It sounded like a great opportunity for me to do something useful, so I jumped at it. I'm not very good at being idle. I don't mind my down time, but I need to be generally productive in some manner or I start feeling useless.

The training was great. They walked us through all the basics of the Marine Corps: what we had available to us, how to handle calls, how to deal with the command of our unit. By the time we finished I think I knew more about the military community life than Paul did.

In March, as we were preparing for our move back to California in May and the birth of our baby girl in June, Paul dropped a bombshell. We had been watching *Wheel of Fortune* one night, and it was Hawaii week. I had been to Hawaii many times, and I loved it. Paul had never been, and I casually mentioned, "Wouldn't it be fun to get stationed in Hawaii sometime." So Paul called me from his school one day and said, "Guess where we're being stationed?"

"Uh, Twentynine Palms," I said hesitantly.

"Nope. Hawaii!"

"What? How? Why?" I couldn't get past one-word questions.

"I bumped into Captain Walker and mentioned that I'd really like to get to Hawaii. Turns out he just got an opening for the base. Its three years, nondeployable . . . and its in Hawaii. What do you think?"

"Uh, wow."

"Aren't you excited? You said you wanted to go to Hawaii."

"I did. I do, I do want to go to Hawaii. I love it there. But, wow. With the baby coming . . . we have family in California. Can I think about it?"

There was silence on the other end of the phone. "Sure you can. We'll talk about it when I get home."

And we did talk about it. We both wanted to go and the idea of him being home for three years with no deployments was a huge temptation. I talked to my mom about it, and she was upset. She was so looking forward to having us close by. In the end we (and by "we" I mean mostly me) decided we wanted to be close to family when the baby was born. So Paul went back to Twentynine Palms knowing that he would have to do a six-month deployment to Okinawa while we were there. All I can say is, it seemed like a good idea at the time.

# Chapter 3

# BRING HER IN
# AT NIGHT

There is a gem of wisdom passed down from veteran Twentynine Palms Marines to incoming Marines. "Bring her in at night." The "her" in question is me, the Marine wife. Bring your wife to Twentynine Palms in the middle of the night so she won't see what she's gotten herself into until the next morning.

Twentynine Palms is well known in the Marine Corps. It's the largest training base in the United States. It's also the largest live-fire base in the Marine Corps. That means Marines can go pretty much anywhere away from Mainside and blow up stuff to their hearts content. The only people to complain are the coyotes. So in terms of training, Twentynine Palms is ideal. For living, Twentynine Palms leaves something to be desired—like civilization. The town of Twentynine Palms is known as an Oasis of Murals because of the myriad murals painted on the sides of nearly every building in the three-stop-light town. It has one grocery store, one discount dollar store, one bar, one drive-in movie theatre, two fast-food restaurants (McDonald's and Burger King), two Chinese food restaurants (both owned by the same family, so I've heard), and seven tattoo parlors. It also has plenty of Joshua trees, scrub brush, tumbleweeds, and its two most defining characteristics, sand and heat. In the summer, temperatures regularly reach 115 degrees. Of course, it's a dry heat. When I cheerily mentioned the fact that "it's a dry heat" to the father of a Marine who had called me for some information on the base he quipped back, "Yeah, so's an oven."

The base itself couldn't be more different from Quantico. Gone are the colonial brick buildings; in their place are buildings that put function over appearance. Which isn't so bad. It makes for good times when giving directions. When I had a friend from college drive out for a visit, the directions I gave him went something like this: stop at the front gate and do everything the guard with the weapon tells you to do, drive straight to the first stoplight and turn left, go past the display of fighter jets and howitzers, keep going past the tanks, turn left at the next light, and go up the hill to our street. If you hit a barbed wire fence you've gone too far.

As huge as the base is, Mainside is actually fairly small. It has the commissary (a brand new one that opened in 2004—it was like getting a Disneyland) and the exchange. There is also a movie theater, a school, a golf course (a requirement for every Marine base), the administrative offices, and two churches. The Protestant and Catholic churches are mirror images of each other and face off across the wide grass expanse of the parade deck. When we first arrived, Paul and I joked that after church services ended we expected to see the congregations spill out and meet in the middle of the lawn for a football reformation grudge match. Never did see that happen.

We left Quantico, drove back across the country, and arrived in Twentynine Palms on May 2, 2002. Paul was going to be the new communications officer for the 3rd Battalion, 4th Marines (Three-Four). Me, I was still pregnant. My advice to anyone considering a cross-country drive is not to do it when you're eight months pregnant. I also learned an important life lesson: when pregnant and driving long distances, never pass up an opportunity to pee. So after stopping at every rest stop along the way and speeding through that southern state that shall not be named, we arrived on my mom's doorstep in Palm Springs.

There weren't any available houses on base for us when we arrived, so my mom let us stay with her until something opened up. It ended up being three months and one baby later before we were able to move on base. Paul had to commute an hour to work every day, which was difficult, and I had to make the drive out to the base hospital for my doctor appointments.

And those doctor appointments became very frequent. By June I had developed preeclampsia. I swelled up so badly I looked like the girl in *Willy Wonka and the Chocolate Factory* who turns into a blueberry, except I wasn't blue (thank heavens for small favors during pregnancy). On June 25 my midwife checked me into the hospital for observation. I was induced the next day, and at 1:10 a.m. on June 27 our daughter, Emily Catherine, was born. Paul was able to be with me the whole time I was in the hospital, and he was granted ten days paternity leave. We left the hospital a few days after Emily was born and all three of us moved back in with Mom.

It turned out to be a blessing that we were staying with my mom during those first few weeks with a newborn. Paul was working crazy hours. He would get up at 4 a.m.

and sometimes not make it back until 8 or 9 p.m. He tried to explain to me about the turnover with the previous communications officer and the problems they were encountering, but I wasn't really listening. I was exhausted and cranky and scared to death. What was I supposed to do with this new baby? The first time I was left alone with Emily for an entire day I cried as much as she did.

Finally in August, a house became available, and we moved on base. Not having to commute made life much easier for Paul. I, however, wasn't too happy about moving on base because it would be another two to three weeks before our furniture would be delivered, and I didn't love the idea of sleeping on the floor for that long. All of our household goods had been packed up when we left Quantico and had been sitting in storage until we could get a house. We had all of Emily's baby gear since we hadn't bought anything big for her until we moved back to California. So at least she would be set up. Honestly though, I was also terrified of leaving the support of my mom. What was I going to do when it was really just me and this tiny baby? When we were getting ready to leave my mom's house, I was a sobbing mess and I didn't want to go. But Paul wanted to stop the long commute.

"Why should I move on base when we don't even have any furniture?" I demanded (and yes I did sound that bad).

Then my mom gave me a wonderful piece of advice that I have remembered ever since. "Because you love him and he asked you to." That shut me up, and we moved into our new base house. We spent two weeks sleeping on the air mattress and sitting on the floor, but I didn't make a scene about it again.

When she was six weeks old, Emily finally started to fall into a bit of a routine, and I was able to translate some of her cries. That all helped to mellow me out a bit; I didn't feel like the worst mother in the world anymore. One of my friends in Quantico had warned me not to make judgments about my new baby or my mothering skills (or lack thereof) until after the first twelve weeks. "It's just like being pregnant," she said. "The first twelve weeks are the worst." She was a wise, wise woman.

Living on a military base is kind of like living in a very small town—or like high school. You know practically everyone in your neighborhood. And the people you don't know someone you know (did you follow that?). It's a tight-knit community where good news travels fast and bad news faster. But you will never find a group of people more willing to help each other. People drop by unexpectedly; babysitting duties are freely exchanged. Each of us knows what the other is going through, and many times we're all in the same boat. As I would come to find out, sometimes it's a blessing to live among women who share your life.

The housing in Twentynine Palms is much nicer than most of Quantico. Not that I didn't have some fond memories of our crack house, but I was looking forward to an upgrade. The housing areas on base at Twentynine Palms are divided by rank. Our house was on the very last street of company-grade officers and across the street from field grade. It was a single-story ranch and a huge step up from Quantico. It was big—well, bigger than our previous crack house—and in great condition. We shared only one wall this time. I met our neighbor, Jenny, over the fence in the backyard. She and her husband Jeff had two kids a few years older than Emily. We chatted, and she welcomed us to the base. Jenny and I spoke a few times off and on, and Paul was happy we had good neighbors again. Then one day he came home from work very pensive.

"What's the matter?" I asked.

"I bumped into our neighbor at work today."

"Who? Jeff?"

"Yep," Paul answered. "Or as I now like to call him, Sir." Turns out, Jeff was a major. Paul, being very big on customs and courtesies (the etiquette of the Marine Corps) never spoke his first name again. As the days went by we met more of our neighbors—Sir and Dawn, Sir and Yvonne, Sir and Terry, and Sir and Amy.

We lucked out in that our neighbors Steve and Justine from Quantico ended up in Twentynine Palms as well. Paul and I were thrilled—Steve and Justine, not so much. Twentynine Palms was not their idea of paradise. Their son, Sam, was six months older than Emily, and the two of them got along really well so we were able to have some fun together. But Steve and Justine were definitely counting the days until it was time to move again. They couldn't believe we came to Twentynine Palms by choice, much less that we had given up Hawaii for it. In fact, no one could believe it.

The drawback to living on base was the loss of my mom's presence. Now we were well and truly in the military life. Paul was working all the time. On the upside he had been promoted to first lieutenant; even though it was Paul's promotion and not mine, it made me feel like less of a rookie wife. There had been a great deal of turnover within the battalion, a new commanding officer (CO), new staff officers, tons of new Marines. There was also growing concern that Three-Four would be one of the first battalions to go if the president decided to send troops into Iraq. So the training schedule was fast and hard. Paul was gone at least ten days out every month, usually more.

When Emily was two months old, my dad and stepmother came to visit us (OK, they really only came to see the baby). Paul was out in the field (again), and Emily was due for her first round of immunizations. I was fully into paranoid-mother mode. My dad ended up coming with me to the doctor's appointment, and to his credit, he didn't laugh when I told the doctor I was afraid Emily was going to contract measles, mumps, rubella, hepatitis, whooping cough, and autism from the vaccinations. After much reassurance, Emily made it through the shots with only a minute of tears and a dose of painkiller. I went home and helped myself to the cookie jar.

As the battalion's training schedule became more intense, my frustration level matched it. Whenever Paul would come home and announce another field exercise or another trip for a planning conference or that he had been given weekend duty—again —I would just want to cry. And I often did. This was not the "it's just another job" I had envisioned when we got married. There were nights I would pace the floor with my crying daughter and curse Paul for choosing this life. Then I would curse myself for talking him out of the Hawaii billet. We could be sitting on a beach sipping mai tais (well, not me, I was still breast-feeding, but I could be sitting on the beach). Paul would probably be home more, and we wouldn't be worrying about Paul possibly going to war—and he would be home more! The truth was I just didn't get it yet. The military isn't a job, it's a life—your only life. Paul couldn't call in sick or explain that he needed to skip a field exercise because his wife was going nuts. He did what he was told—that was his job: follow orders, give orders, and take care of his Marines. My job was not to kill him in the process. I didn't have a lot of other options, and that feeling of helplessness was really hard for me to accept.

The best thing that happened during those early months was my involvement with Three-Four's Key Volunteer Network (KVN). It actually happened even before Emily was born. Paul took me to base to see his new office and to meet some of the people with whom he would be working. One of the Marines I met was Major Matt Baker, the battalion's executive officer (XO). He was a tall man, handsome with a great smile. If GQ did a Marine issue, he could be the cover boy. It was a Saturday, and he was dressed in slacks and a polo shirt. He even had his dog in the office. Rowdy was a tiny, furry purse dog—

you know, the ones that ride along in a purse with only their little heads peeking out. I instantly loved Rowdy because even though I was nearly nine months pregnant he still managed to find my lap and jump into it.

Major Baker welcomed me easily, told me to call him Matt, and asked after the baby. He was also the family readiness officer for the battalion. That means he was in charge of making sure the KVN ran smoothly and had everything it needed. At the moment, it desperately needed volunteers, so I volunteered. Actually, I think Paul told him I had been through the training, and I was summarily volunteered. Not that I minded, I liked Major Baker, and I thought it would be a good use of my time. (Remember, I didn't have arms full of infant yet.)

In September, about a month after we moved on base, the KVN hosted a Spouse Appreciation Night. This get-together was meant to introduce all the wives to the commanding officer, the executive officer, and all the Key Volunteers (KVs). It was also a very thinly veiled recruiting event—we needed more volunteers. It was going to be my first chance to meet the women who would come to fill my life for the next three years.

I was surprisingly nervous about meeting the other volunteers, and I showed up early to meet the KVs before all the wives showed up. When I arrived at the base community center I was stunned by the frenetic activity. Food was being prepared, sign-in tables were being set up, and people were laughing and talking all at once. I didn't even know who to introduce myself to. Every once in a while I would spot a Marine in cammies lifting tables or chairs at the direction of the KVs or wisely stepping out of the way of a woman on a mission.

One of these Marines was Major Baker. Fortunately he both remembered me and noticed me standing there looking vaguely lost. He came up and helped me make the rounds of introductions. His wife, Ann, was the KV advisor, the leader of the group. This is normally a position filled by the wife of the commanding officer, but our new CO was married to an army officer who was stationed in Virginia. Like me, I think Ann was volunteered for the assignment. It was her first time in the job, but she jumped in with both feet. Ann was a Midwestern girl who should have been born in New York. She was stylish and poised from her swept-up blonde hair to her brightly painted toes. (At that point, I was just thrilled to be seeing my toes again!) She welcomed me warmly and then rushed off to organize the door prizes.

I stayed generally out of the way after I met all the KVs. Eventually wives started to show up. They all stopped at the sign-in table. Turns out part of the bribery—uh, incentive—for the wives to show up was the promise of the next day off for any Marine whose wife attended the event. I asked Paul if that meant he got a day off too. He just smirked and said, "No way."

This was my first experience with an entire battalion of wives. There was quite a mix. We had eighteen- and nineteen-year-old wives who showed in hip-hugger jeans and Britney Spears belly-bearing shirts; some complete with belly-button rings and thongs pulling up out of the back of their jeans. Then we had the older, more seasoned wives wearing their conservative slacks and shoes and looking like they had already seen everything the Marine Corps could throw at them. And we had everyone in between. We had Caucasian, African-American, Hispanic, Asian, young, old, with kids, without kids. I remember being suddenly struck that we were looking at a microcosm of society in one room.

After everyone got settled into our big circle of chairs—like a grown-up campfire—Major Baker stepped forward. He thanked everyone for coming and handled the introductions. When he was finished, the new commanding officer stepped up: Lieutenant Colonel Bryan P. McCoy. If ever one man fit the phrase "commanding officer" to a T, it was Lieutenant Colonel McCoy. He was solid and even taller than Major Baker. I would find out later that he runs fifty-mile endurance races—for fun! He had that kind of presence you remember your elementary school principal having—like the only thing more intimidating than being in his office was the fact that he could call your parents. I had no way of knowing then that he was one of the finest officers in the Marine Corps and that in a matter of months he would lead my husband into battle.

In spite of his no-nonsense Marine presence, he was very warm and open with us. He and Major Baker passed out carnations to all of the wives and part of me wondered how they had reacted when that plan had been proposed. But they did it with a smile.

After the CO and XO did their part, Ann got up to

speak about the KVN. She gave an overview of what we did and what services we could provide, and then she introduced all of us by name and company. I stood when she introduced me and felt a little presumptuous because I hadn't actually done anything yet. Nobody seemed to care, though. That is one of the best things about military life. No matter where you have come from or how new you are to the base, you can just step right in. It comes from all of us learning that in the Marine Corps, people can come and go quickly. Often, no sooner do you make a friend then he or she ends up being transferred to Okinawa. In order to keep sane in this transitory kind of life, you have to learn to welcome people as soon as they walk in the door and be able to say good-bye to others just as quickly. It's one of the aspects of this crazy life I love. When you meet someone new there's not much time for small talk and the lengthy process of getting to know each other. It's like speed dating for friends.

"Where did you come from?" (Translation: "At which base were you last stationed?")

"Who's your husband with?" ("To what unit is your husband assigned?")

"Do you have any kids?" ("Can we arrange a play date for our children?")

Military life moves fast, and you have to jump in just to keep up. The good news is that everyone else has just jumped in as well.

All in all, the Spouse Appreciation Night went well.

There were door prizes to give away (more bribery, I would find out later), and at the end of the evening it was question and answer time. Wives who had been hearing the rumors of a possible deployment to Iraq put Lieutenant Colonel McCoy on the spot.

"Ladies," he said diplomatically. "Right now everything you're hearing is rumor and speculation. We don't know any more than you do at the moment. If something comes up and we have to deploy, we will get you the information as soon as we can. For right now, find out who your Key Volunteer is and keep her phone number handy in case you have any questions."

That last little tidbit nearly made me swallow my gum. These women were going to call me? I didn't know anything. What had I gotten myself into?

I found out pretty quickly. The KVN held monthly meetings, and I made it to the next one. As soon as I stepped in the door, I was just swept along in the momentum. It was kind of like joining a race halfway through—just follow everyone else and try to keep up. Ann Baker was standing beside Krista Boyce, the battalion's KV coordinator. Traditionally, the advisor is more of an overseer for the group, while the coordinator handles most of the administrative and organizational duties. Krista was the wife of the Weapons Company commander and had already been through the last Okinawa deployment with Three-Four. She was also six months pregnant with their first child. I liked Krista immediately; she was organized, efficient, and had the slightest touch of South Carolina in her voice.

Also in the group was Misty Thompson. A Marine sergeant herself, she had to walk a difficult line between being a Marine wife and being a Marine. Monica Coughlin was, like me, new to the group. She had a no-nonsense, rough exterior that boarded on abrasive, and it took a while to get to know her. Mary Pittman was the youngest of the group and still feeling her way around military life. Kristy Hayes had three adorable little girls, and Erika Norton was a poised professional woman.

And then there were the lieutenants' wives. We were like a political body unto ourselves. Besides me, there were five other women. Jennifer Johnston was a true Texas girl—confident and brutally honest, she pulled no punches and let you know loud and clear if you did something right and louder and clearer if something was wrong. I tried once to call her Jenny, but it just didn't fit. Stephanie Dillbeck lived right across the street from Jennifer on base. Stephanie had two children, short brown hair, and the most positive perspective on life. Her husband, Frank, worked with Jennifer's husband, Tony. (The two of them had quite the reputation for insanity, but they would both distinguish themselves in the coming months.) Jessica Wessman reminded me of the homecoming queen. She was petite, blonde, and forever in high heels. (Thanks to her influence, most of my shoes are now heels.) Lynde Phillips was the outdoor girl of the group. She worked as a trail guide in Joshua Tree National Park and had spent months backpacking around

Australia while her husband, Jay, had been on the last deployment. Monica Langella was a nurse who lived over an hour away, but she still commuted every month for the KVN meetings.

I spent the most time talking to Jennifer. She was the KV company coordinator for Headquarters and Service Company (H&S Company). Each infantry battalion is divided into smaller companies. Most of them are line companies, the actual rifle toting, go-in-and-shoot-stuff guys. Weapons Company covers the large weapons. H&S Company is basically everything else: the command, logistics, motor transport, supply, and communications. It's usually the largest company of Marines. The possible deployment was central to the KV meeting. It was on everybody's mind. We kept saying, "Hopefully they won't go, hopefully everything will work out, but just in case, let's plan for the worst." We planned on getting a newsletter out to the families once a month during a deployment, rather than once a quarter as it usually went out when the guys are home. Many of these KV women had already been with the battalion for a year or so; their husbands had already gone on an Okinawa deployment and had just returned in February. We also talked about planning another social event for the wives—deployment or not. We planned a Christmas party for the beginning of December, and Major Baker, who attended the meeting as our Marine contact, was volunteered to dress up as Santa.

We were given homework as well: we needed to call all the wives and introduce ourselves, make sure we had their correct address for the newsletter, give them our phone number, and answer any questions they might have. Jennifer and I split the H&S wives roster between the two of us. I told her I'd like to have the section with the communications platoon because those were Paul's Marines. Calling them all sounded simple enough until I realized I had sixty wives on my list. But then, so did Jennifer. There were 120 wives in H&S, and Jennifer and I were the only volunteers from the company.

The only other social outlet I had at the time was the Officers' Spouses' Club (OSC). Every base has one. It's a social group for—just as it says—the wives of officers stationed at on the base. The club's first social was held in September as well. I've come to realize that most everything on base correlates to the school year. Activities start in the fall and end before summer vacation. The Twentynine Palms OSC operates in three ways. First, it hosts a big monthly event—maybe a lunch or an evening of bingo (yes, you read that correctly, bingo). The culminating event is the Mardi Gras benefit auction to raise money for its philanthropic fund. Second, the club also sponsors a bunch of smaller subgroups: a book club, a hiking club, a play group, a cooking club, and a bunco club (don't ask me to explain the game, it's not my thing). Finally, each unit on base has a unit representative who's responsible for organizing coffees for the wives of the unit.

Now you may be asking yourself, what's a coffee? Think of it more as a gathering of wives. Often it is centered on coffee, but just as often it can be a lunch thing, or a game night, or a wine tasting. After I joined the OSC I found out that Jennifer Johnston was Three-Four's representative. She asked later if I wanted to help coordinate things, but we never had a good turnout. Our wives didn't like coffee, I guess. Eventually we just gave up on it. When the president of the OSC wanted to know why our unit didn't seem to do much within the OSC, Jennifer and I tried to explain that the "coffee concept" just didn't work with our wives. Turns out Three-Four has always been something of a renegade unit—both the Marines and the wives. I don't know why that tradition continues through changes of command and new Marines, but Three-Four has always done things just a little bit differently than everyone else.

In the end, I got more socialization and more company just in random places on base than in these official groups. Going to the commissary usually turned into a social event because I'd bump into people and we'd stop to chat among the lettuce. Or I'd bump into a friend or two while on my daily walks with Emily.

At the time, the gym on base didn't have child care (a fact that led to a crusade of mine a few years later; read on), and I wasn't ready to leave Emily with a sitter so I could go work out. I finally told Paul that if he wanted a sane wife he needed to get some fitness equipment so I could work out at home. We ended up with a really nice setup in the garage. I put Emily's playpen out there with a television and popped in a *Baby Einstein* video. She'd happily watch the dancing puppets, and I could get in an hour's workout. That was a good system, and I credit my home gym with keeping me from losing my mind.

In December, Paul and I planned a Christmas party for his platoon. I spent three days cooking and baking. We held the party in one of the radio cages (a big, industrial room filled with radios, computers, and everything else I don't want to touch) in the communications shop. There were brownies, cookies, cheesecakes—it was a dentist's nightmare. But it was also a lot of fun. I had already gotten to know many of the wives of Paul's Marines through my KV phone calls. I never stated explicitly that Paul was the platoon commander (translation: their husband's boss), but most of them figured it out or their husbands told them later. The Christmas party gave me a chance to meet the Marines as well. That was fun, kind of like being a den mother. No one ever called me by my first name—I was always Ma'am or Mrs. Keener. I've told a number of my civilian friends that when I married a Marine not only did my last name change, but my first name did too. I went from Michelle to Ma'am with a single "I do."

Eventually, with Emily growing older, we all fell into a routine that worked pretty well. Paul was still working a lot, but I guess I got used to it. I had my days with Emily all scheduled. By six months she was a changed child—so much easier—or maybe I was just getting used to her. Every once in a while when Paul was in the field for a long time, or if Emily was having a particularly bad day I would slip back into Frazzled Wife mode, but we were doing OK. I was losing my pregnancy weight, which always makes things brighter, and Paul was settling into his new job.

There was still talk of war and Three-Four going to Iraq, but like the armed patrols back at Quantico after September 11, I became sort of numb to it. For a long time we were sure he would be gone before Thanksgiving and then before Christmas, but nothing happened. It took too much energy to think about it constantly, so eventually I just stopped worrying about it. It was always there, in the back of my mind, in conversations with other wives. Paul was convinced they were going, but then again, he'd been saying that since September. It just seemed too farfetched, like a plot for a movie. How could my husband really go to war? Sure it's a possibility. But a reality? My mind just couldn't conceive of it. I couldn't imagine what it would be like, so it never seemed real.

Until January 24, 2003.

# Chapter 4

# HERE WE GO

In December of 2002, a warning order was posted for Three-Four. This was essentially an official warning to the battalion that if troops were sent to Iraq then Three-Four would be at the top of the list. But no date had been set, and it still wasn't a certainty that the United States was going into Iraq. There was still a chance that Saddam Hussein would have a radical change of heart, and that no troops would be sent to Iraq at all.

Honestly, there weren't many of us in Twentynine Palms who thought that war could be avoided. So when the warning order came out, it brought a sense of inevitability of Paul being deployed, but without a set date it didn't change much of our daily life. Everything was a possibility: they could be deploying, they could be going in a week, or a month, or never. I remember being incredibly grateful that he was home for Emily's first Christmas and praying every night that nothing would come of the warning order.

There was nothing particularly special about January 24, 2003. Paul got up early and left for work, and I stayed in bed until Emily woke up. It was a normal morning for us. Emily and I had breakfast and settled down on the family-room floor for some play-time. She had just started crawling at Christmas and was fascinated by her newly discovered locomotion.

At about 9 a.m., Paul walked in the front door. It wasn't at all like him to come home for anything in the middle of the workday. He walked in without smiling and stood in the doorway leading to the kitchen. I knew something was wrong.

"What's going on?" I asked.

"The deployment order came down today. We're going." He didn't need to say where—we both knew where he was going.

I could feel my heart knocking against my ribs. *Oh my God. He's going to war. This is it.* "When?"

"I'm on the first plane. I leave tonight."

"Tonight?"

Even now I can remember the fear that tightened my throat. Here we were standing in our family room, calmly discussing my husband leaving for war that night while our baby crawled around our feet.

"How long will you be gone?"

*What if he doesn't come back?*

"They told us to prepare for a year."

*I can't do this. Tell him he can't go.*

"OK. So what do we do now?"

At that point my husband had one of the better ideas of his life—he put his arms around me. I kept telling myself to be strong, not to scream or cry. There was no going back now. I just wanted to stay strong in front of Paul. I knew he was hurting too. He could be missing a year out of his daughter's life—he could be missing the rest of her life. I didn't want to make it any harder for him, but there was an actual physical pain in my heart as we held each other. I know I cried. He told me it would be all right, that everything would be fine, but we both knew they were empty words. We had less than a day left to spend together. When he picked up Emily and held her close, I thought I would snap. How could my baby's daddy be going into harm's way? How did this happen? When would it end?

As busy as the day was, we wanted to spend as much time together as possible, but it wouldn't be easy. Paul called my mom and told her what was happening and asked her to come out to watch Emily for us. She made it out to base in record time. Paul called his mom and sister and told them he was going, and I called my dad. We didn't tell anyone else though. Neither us were up for a flood of phone calls that day. I planned to let everyone know what had happened after he was gone.

I'd like to say we had a movie scene type of day: going to the park, holding hands, saying long and poetic good-byes. As with most things, though, military life is not a movie. Paul had a ton of things to do to get ready to leave. He was only able to spend a few minutes at home after he gave me the news. Then he had to go pick up his gear, get his Marines ready, and take care of outstanding business. I stopped him before he left and took a picture of him holding Emily. The photo shows him in his desert cammies, her in her pink pajamas, blissfully unaware of the importance of the picture. I said it was for the scrapbook, but we both knew it was in case he didn't come back. I also took a picture of Paul alone. After he left, I taped it to the wall next to Emily's changing table so she could look at her daddy every day.

A few hours later—and believe me I was watching every hour tick away—Paul came back home. My mom stayed with Emily, and I went with Paul on some of his errands. The first one was the worst. He had to go get his gas mask fixed. He had found a small break in the seal and needed to get it repaired before going. At the time we were expecting chemical-weapons attacks in Iraq, and the gas mask was the only thing that could save him in a chemical or biological attack. Only a few months earlier he'd received the much-debated anthrax vaccination.

I waited in the car while Paul went in to drop off his gas mask. I tried not to think about what he was getting and why he needed it. By this time I was over the initial tears and had become somewhat numbed by it all. Even now I can't really explain the swiftly changing emotions we went through. After all the months of uncertainty and anxiety, it was time for action. I think it's a bit like having a major medical test done. The days of waiting for the results are tense and draining, and eventually you get to the point where even a bad result would be better than the not knowing. And once you have your answer, you just move on to the treatment, even if the treatment sucks.

That day, we were rushing to get things done, and there wasn't any time to dwell or cry or be poetic. After getting a new gas mask, we went to the base exchange. Paul wanted to get a new wedding ring. He had lost weight since our wedding day, and his wedding band was loose. He didn't want to lose it in Iraq, but he didn't want to go to combat without a wedding band. There was no time to have his ring sized, so we bought a new one. It was just a plain, medium-width gold band. We were standing in the middle of a crowded store when he took off the ring I had given him two years before and asked me to keep it safe for him. We didn't even bother with a box for the new one. I put it on his finger right there in front of the saleslady.

After the ring, we had to get supplies. Paul needed batteries, socks, Chapstick, soap, bug spray, a new towel, shower shoes, toothpaste, trash bags, laundry detergent— all the ridiculously daily things you never associate with war. I insisted on extra sunscreen, writing paper, envelopes, and stamps. Paul at one point asked me to go find a plastic box for his soap. I came back with a bright purple one, and he just shook his head; I guessed purple didn't fit the macho-Marine image. I didn't know it at the time, but every time he sent me off to go find something he was grabbing cards for Emily and me, for Valentine's Day, birthdays, our anniversary—even though all those events were months away. He was afraid it might be his last chance to get cards, and he didn't want those days to pass and have me think he had forgotten.

By the time we returned home, the daylight was fading. There was a strange surreal quality to the rest of the day. Paul was packing his sea bag, my mom was watching Emily, and I was baking cookies. I didn't know what else to do. I baked cookies for him and his Marines to take on the plane. Eventually I made dinner, and we all sat at the table like it was any other night, not the last time we would all be together for God only knew how long.

Paul and I didn't talk that day about the possibility of him being killed. In the months leading up to the deployment we had talked about it enough. Paul had taken out a second insurance policy, given me power of attorney (POA), and had written his will. That day we tried not to talk about it. But it was there, the proverbial elephant in the living room.

When it was time for Emily to go to sleep he took her into her bedroom, and I cried knowing these were the last few moments he had with her before he left. Deep down I was crying because I was afraid they might be the last moments he had with her at all. What if he didn't come back? Emily wouldn't remember him. She wouldn't remember how much he loved her. How he tossed her up in the air until she giggled. That he had been the first person to hold her. That he had changed her first diaper. She had changed his life the moment she was born, and if he didn't come back, she would never know it. He wouldn't even be a memory to her. That just wasn't fair.

Unfortunately Emily was used to me putting her to bed, and she cried most of the time Paul was with her. I finally went back and took over the task. I was holding Emily as Paul kissed her one last time and said he loved her more than anything. I rocked Emily longer than I needed to that night. My life was normal when I held her and soothed her to sleep. As long as I was rocking her, life was going on as it should. As soon as I put her in her crib and shut the door, I would be faced again with the chaos of war.

It was midnight when my mom said good night. There were more tears and hugs. She had two parting thoughts for Paul: "I love you. Don't do anything stupid."

The buses were picking up the Marines at 6 a.m. the next day. There had been a short delay with his flight, so we had an extra few hours together. But Paul still had to pick up his weapon from the armory and pack up some of his computer stuff from the office. A little after 1 a.m. he said he had finished packing and was ready to leave. I added a few things to his bag. I put a pair of Emily's tiny socks in a Ziploc bag. I asked if he wanted one of her teddy bears, but that got vetoed like the purple soap holder. But he did take the socks. I also gave him a second Ziploc bag with a handkerchief that I had sprayed with my perfume, some pictures of all of us to take with him, and the cookies I had made earlier.

As he was getting ready to leave I told him I was going to meet him at the buses just before 6 a.m. He said I didn't have to, but I wasn't ready to say good-bye yet. When he left for his office, I tried to sleep for a few hours. My alarm went off at 5 a.m., and I was anything but rested. I stared into my closet for a long time wondering what to wear. I finally went for jeans and a sweater and put some effort into putting on makeup.

My mom was in the guest room and would wake up with Emily, so I drove down to Paul's office. The buses were waiting in the large parking lot outside his building when I got there. There were Marines patrolling the area and sea bags stacked in organized piles around the lot. I found my way to Paul's office and went in.

My husband was gone and in his place was a warrior. He was in uniform, his weapon in its holster strapped to his leg. He put his arms around me and held me for a long time. When he let me go, I knew his mind was already on the coming battles. We didn't have much time left. He put on his flak jacket and grabbed his sea bag, backpack, and helmet. As we walked out to the waiting buses he asked me to wait by the building. He crossed the barbed wire barricade and dropped off his stuff. He stopped and spoke to some of his Marines before coming back to me.

"You should go home," he said as he held my hands. "It's cold."

"But I want to stay until you go." *Was this really it? How had it come so fast? Isn't there so much more for us to say?*

"I can't wait here with you. I've got to go make sure my Marines are ready. I don't want you to just stand around in the cold. Go home to Emily." Paul has never been good at good-byes. He doesn't like to linger over them, he doesn't like to draw out the sadness. I should have expected it, but somehow I thought that this time everything should be different. Where was the dramatic music, the brilliant setting sun? This wasn't glamorous. This just hurt.

"OK." This was what he had to do now—put the welfare of his Marines first. He had a responsibility to them and that took priority. I knew that and it was time to let go. "I love you. Please be safe."

He smiled a little at that. "I'm a Marine."

"I know . . . be safe anyway." We held each other one last time. "I love you." The words seemed so small. They didn't convey all the feelings and thoughts, everything you suddenly realize you want to make another person understand. But he knew.

"I love you, too. Take care of Emily and tell her I love her."

And that was it. He kissed me again, then he turned around and walked away. He never looked back.

I stood there watching him for a few minutes. He was all business, and I knew I had to go. So I got in my car and drove away. It was 5:40 a.m. and the buses were leaving for the airfield at 6 a.m. I cried and prayed the whole way home.

When I got there I picked up Emily and held her tight until she started squirming and wanted down—5:50 a.m.—Paul was still at the parking lot. He was still on base. How could I feel so alone when he was still so close?

It was 5:55 a.m., and I entertained wild ideas about racing to the parking lot and catching him for one last dramatic embrace before he went to war. One last attempt for the movie moment, the dramatic scene before the hero goes off to war. Something, anything to make this feel more romantic, more unreal so it wouldn't actually be my life, so it wouldn't hurt as much. Instead, I made oatmeal for Emily, and put on coffee for my mom. In the movies, they never show what the heroine does once the plane leaves. All the mundane bits of daily life that still need to be done—even when your husband goes to war.

As I poured myself a glass of water and got Emily in her high chair, I glanced at the clock. 6:01 a.m. He was gone.

# Chapter 5

# SETTING HOME FIRES

Murphy's Law states, "Anything that can go wrong, will go wrong." Only a few hours after Paul left, I became a firm believer in the military version of Murphy's Law: "Anything that can go wrong, will go wrong as soon as your husband deploys." It's a running joke with military wives that nothing breaks until after the husband is gone. One wife I know swears that her washing machine is in a conspiracy with the Marine Corps. It knows the moment her husband deploys and deliberately breaks down each and every time. Maybe it's just that we don't notice all the little, and not so little, things our husbands do for us when they're around. Maybe stuff is always going wrong, but we don't think much of it because we know we have someone to share it with, someone we can count on to repair it, explain it, or replace it.

For me, it was the car. The night before Paul left, he drove his truck to his office, and my mom and I planned to go back the next morning and drive it home. So when I'd pulled myself together after saying good-bye to Paul, we got ready to go. We didn't even make it into the car— I had a flat tire, the first one, ever. OK, now what? Now I call my husband and say, "Honey, can you fix my tire?" He says, "Sure, be right there." Then he puts on his car-working clothes (a grungy pair of jeans and work shirt from his merchant-marine days), goes outside for a while then comes back in saying "OK, all done." That's how car problems work in our house. (Coincidentally that's also how computer problems work.)

But not this time. Now I was in charge of car problems. Standing in my driveway staring stupidly at the tire,

I suddenly remembered that movie *Speed*. When the bad guy has a bomb set to go off, he asks the cocky Keanu Reeves character, "What do you do? What do you do?" Good question. Fortunately, I had a plan. It was called the auto club. Not bad, huh?

I never actually had to call AAA. Instead, one of Paul's staff sergeants changed the tire for me.

The single Marines living in the barracks had to have all of their stuff packed up and moved out of their rooms while they were deployed. That way the rooms would be available in case any other Marines needed them. That's the military for you—nothing goes to waste. Staff Sergeant Musau Mutua asked if he could leave some of his things with us so that when he returned he wouldn't have to wait for the Marine Corps to deliver it all back to him. Well, his flight ended up being delayed, and he needed shoes other than his boots to wear while he waited. (The man was planning to go to war, so he hadn't put his loafers in his sea bag.) He called and asked if he could pick them up. When I gave him directions I flippantly described our house as, "It's the house with the Mazda with a flat tire in the driveway."

Not much later, Staff Sergeant Mutua showed up, and we found his shoes. Then he offered to change the tire for me. At first I felt bad about it, that didn't seem like much of a way for him to spend his last day before going to war. But he said—and I will never forget this—"The lieutenant takes good care of us, this is the least I can do for him." I had never really thought of my husband as a platoon commander before. Sure I knew what he looked like in his uniform, but he was always just Paul. Now, talking to Staff Sergeant Mutua, I got a glimpse of the other side of my husband. He really was a Marine.

So I took my piece of humble pie and let him get to work. Of course I didn't have the right tool for taking off the tire bolts. He ended up going across the street to Sir and Yvonne's house to borrow a tire iron. I had spoken only two sentences to Yvonne before that day, but we chatted for a few minutes in the middle of the street while Staff Sergeant Mutua put on the spare tire.

After putting on the spare, he even offered to drive me to the garage and then pick up Paul's truck on the way back. I passed and told him to go enjoy what was left of his day. He said he'd be by later to drop off the shoes again before he left. He actually came by three more times that day. He dropped off the shoes when his flight was rescheduled. He showed up at the door in his uniform, weapon strapped to his side, and I was amazed again at the transformation these men undergo when the battlefield calls. Of course the flight was delayed again, so he came back and picked up some other things, thinking he'd have an extra day.

I went back to baking. Cookies seemed like the least I could do to say thank you for changing the tire. But that's me—when in doubt, bake. Throughout the course of the two deployments I gained quite a reputation for my baked goods. I used to joke that I baked to keep Paul in the good graces of the command. I figured it was hard to yell at a guy who had just passed around a plate of homemade brownies. I planned to have the cookies ready by the next morning for Staff Sergeant Mutua when he came by again to drop off his stuff.

The next morning came and went, and no Staff Sergeant Mutua. I finally went outside to get the mail, and I saw his suitcases sitting on our front porch. He'd left a note saying he left early that morning; he didn't want to risk waking the baby by ringing the doorbell, so he just left his stuff outside. He never got his cookies.

I, however, got a surprise the next day when I took the car to the garage to have the tire fixed. I bumped into my neighbor Jenny from next door. We stopped and chatted for a bit when she suddenly asked the strangest thing.

"So, I heard you had your . . . ," she paused as if searching for the right word. "brother out for a visit?"

Brother? I have a stepbrother who lives in northern California, but he hadn't been down to Twentynine Palms yet. So in genuine confusion, I replied, "My brother? No. My mom is visiting, though. That's her car." Maybe she didn't know who owned the blue Dodge parked in the street.

"Oh no, I knew that," Jenny said. "I thought I heard you had a man visiting you a lot yesterday."

Ahh, understanding began to dawn. Perhaps I should mention here that I am a small, white girl who can't even get a tan, and Staff Sergeant Mutua is a well-built African-American man.

"No, that was one of Paul's Marines," I say.

"Oh." Now, you may have caught on to her meaning

earlier, but it wasn't until that "Oh" that it finally clicked in my brain where she was going with these questions. I didn't know if I should be insulted that she thought I began a hot affair the day my husband left for Iraq or if I should be flattered that she thought I could move that fast. Then I realized Jenny hadn't seen Staff Sergeant Mutua and I together, so she must have gotten the word from someone else. Suddenly, my street reminded me of a high school hallway—how much gossip had spread in just one day? Ordinarily I might not have bothered to explain. I might have let the rumors circulate and just enjoyed the show. But this time I had a terrible fear that somehow word would get back to Paul that his wife was sleeping with every Marine left on base. I didn't want that in his head when he was going into combat.

"We're storing some of his things for him during the deployment," I said. "He was dropping off some stuff and then changed a flat tire for me."

"Ohhhh." This "Oh" had an entirely different quality—the relief that she wasn't living next to a cheating wife, I guess. Now I was getting a little ticked off, but instead of saying something snotty I left for the garage.

I mentioned the conversation to Jennifer Johnston later, and she laughed. Looking back I know its funny, and even Paul laughed when I told him about it. I also told him not to mention it to Staff Sergeant Mutua, who would feel terrible, but I'm sure Paul did anyway.

To be honest, during the deployment I knew wives who were cheating. I wasn't close to any of them, but again—like high school—everyone knew. It seemed like such a rotten thing to do. It's bad enough to cheat when your husband is working down the road, but when he's in a war zone? That's low. That will end my soapbox on infidelity—but don't worry, I have others.

My mom left the following day. She had a trip, but she promised to come back in a few weeks. Now it was truly just Emily, me, and the worry. The battalion had flown into Kuwait and set up camp near the Iraqi border. There they waited. The whole world was waiting, really. What was going to happen? My television set was on the Fox News channel all day, every day. Fortunately, Emily was only seven months old, and I don't think she cared that news anchor Shepard Smith was my new best friend. No matter what I was doing, one ear was always listening for some news. When would the war start?

Just days after Paul left, the president gave the State of the Union address. Jennifer called me the day before and said she was going to be interviewed by a Palm Springs news broadcast for her reaction to the president's speech. She asked if I would be willing to be interviewed as well. OK, why not? The night of the speech, I took Emily over to Jennifer's house—she lived on base just a few streets down—to watch the speech and wait for the reporter. Lynde was there, as well, but she refused to do the interview. She was terrified she'd say something stupid. Of course, once she said that I was convinced I was going to put my foot in my mouth as soon as the little red light on the camera came on.

Fortunately, Jennifer had the foresight to call the base public affairs office, and they sent over Marine Sergeant Jenny Haskamp for support.

The news team showed up a few minutes into the speech and set up. They took some camera footage of us watching the speech on TV. Jennifer, Lynde, and I looked engrossed, and Emily chewed on a ring of plastic keys. When Emily starting getting fussy (there's only so much politics my baby could handle), I started to leave. The reporter, a pretty and aggressive brunette whose name I can't remember, asked if we could do the interview before I left. Sure, why not?

She set me up in front of this wooden American flag plaque on Jennifer's wall. I was standing there holding Emily when the camera turned on and she stuck her microphone in my face.

"So what is your husband's name and what does he do?"

"Lieutenant Paul Keener, he's the communications officer for Three-Four." Hey, I knew those answers. As long as Emily cooperates, we'll be fine.

"And he's deployed, is that correct?"

"Yes, he just left on Saturday."

"And how do you feel, knowing he may be in harm's way?" I know everyone laughs when we see the sports reporter ask the boxer who just lost the big fight, "How do you feel?" "I feel like I got beat up and still didn't win." I didn't realize how stupid the question really sounded until someone asked me.

"It's hard knowing he's in danger. I worry about him every day, but I am so proud of him and the work he is doing." *Good. Proud Marine wife; can't go wrong with that.*

"So, what did you think of the president's speech? Do you support his decision to send troops to Iraq?"

*Uhhh, don't say anything stupid.* "I believe the president is acting in the best interests of the country. He has surrounded himself with experts, and I believe he has carefully considered the evidence presented to him. I believe the president takes very seriously the responsibility he has to the men and women of our armed forces serving overseas, and I don't believe for a second that he is doing this without having considered all of his options." *Ha! That was good.* Out of the corner of my eye I could see Lynde give me a thumbs up sign. OK, I can do this.

"What specifically did the president say tonight that persuaded you to support his decision?"

*I was holding a squirming baby—do you think I can remember anything specific?*

"The evidence that they had found traces of specific chemical weapons and the presence of storage facilities. That was very persuasive." *Ouch, not so good. Please don't use that clip on the air.*

"One last question." *Please let it be something I can answer without sounding stupid.* "How do you feel about all the Iraqi children who will be killed if our troops go into Iraq?"

*Bitch! I'm standing here holding my baby in my arms, and you ask me that?*

Before I could open my mouth to respond, Sergeant Haskamp stepped in and told the reporter it was an inappropriate question. Which was definitely a good thing. My first response would not have been in keeping with the highest traditions of ladylike behavior. The camera kept rolling. Jennifer and Lynde asked me if I was OK. Reporter lady defended herself, saying she just wanted my opinion on a possible war. Sergeant Haskamp wanted the camera to stop rolling; it didn't.

Barely a minute passed when I found my voice again. "I'll answer the question."

Everyone turned to me.

"The children of Iraq have lived in fear for decades," I said. "Saddam Hussein has tortured and killed their parents, deprived them of their childhoods. What better cause can there be than to give the children of Iraq the opportunity to live in freedom and to grow up in safety." *Take that!*

"OK, I've got all I need. Thanks."

The camera shut off. Reporter lady asked for my name and Emily's name, and our contact information in case she wanted to do a follow-up story. Then she sat on the couch and interviewed Jennifer.

Both Lynde and Sergeant Haskamp came over to tell me I did a great job. Then the sergeant told me I shouldn't have mentioned the specific day Paul left—loose lips sink ships and all that. It was a rookie mistake, and I was embarrassed. But everyone liked the way I handled the last question, and no one could believe she had asked such a thing.

I went home pretty soon after that to put Emily to bed. Then I called my mom and asked her to tape the news broadcast. We had satellite television and didn't get the local Palm Springs channels. It would be a few days before I would actually see the report, but the next morning I got a call from Paul.

The battalion was set up in the middle of the desert. There weren't any pay phones, and cell phones weren't allowed for security reasons. But the battalion did have several satellite phones. They were secured lines, but the reception wasn't always good and the connection would cut out for no reason. It wasn't out of the ordinary to say only three or four words before the signal was lost and all you heard was "Please hang up and try again." The satellite phones were frustrating, but we all lived for those calls. The Marines had to take turns using the phones to call home. Paul, though, being the communications officer (the guy in charge of the phones), had one assigned to him. Most of the time he was passing the phone around to his Marines, but I know I was lucky in the amount of calls I got. "Hey, I heard you made the news last night," he said that morning.

"You're in Kuwait. How did you see the Palm Springs news? I haven't even seen it yet."

"Oh, the public affairs office called the rear party about it, and they mentioned it to Lieutenant Colonel McCoy when he called back." (The rear party was made up of the Marines in Three-Four who remained behind in Twentynine Palms to make sure everything back here with the battalion ran smoothly.)

"Lieutenant Colonel McCoy knows?"

"He's the one who told me. He said you and Jennifer did great."

"Wow. I just didn't want to say anything dumb."

"I'm proud of you, honey."

We were able to talk for a few more minutes, and I told him about the rest of the interview, including the Iraqi children question. He had the same reaction I did. In the end, the reporter didn't even use my response to that question. She used what I said about the president's responsibility to the service members and my-less-than-eloquent answer about the chemical weapons. That interview turned out to be a foreshadowing of the love-hate relationship I would develop with the media.

Over the next few weeks, Emily and I fell into a new routine. It's a strange thing that happens during a deployment. Your husband leaves and for the first two or three weeks you don't know what to do with yourself. Nothing seems to make sense, and the prospect of spending month after month without him seems so impossible that you want to break something (usually something of your husband's). Then after about a month, things start to fall into place. As heartless as it sounds, you get used to him being gone. As you make it through each day, the impossible becomes possible. You can live on your own and still get everything done. It may not be as easy, it may not be as fun, but it's doable. And if you look hard enough you can even find some silver linings to the deployment. Maybe you finally start some project or a hobby that you didn't have time for when he was home. For me, there was a lot less housework. I love and adore my husband, but the man is a walking mess. (Though he swears he is organized and neat at work, all I know is when he's home, I clean a lot more.)

So by the end of February, Emily and I were doing OK. The news was on less in my house, and my days were relatively predictable. Until the week I affectionately refer to as "the week from hell."

It all started with Emily getting sick. She had always been a healthy child—she'd never even had a cold or an ear infection. But out of nowhere she came down with something flu-like. And by flu-like I mean she was projectile puking all over me, the carpet, the chairs, and her crib. There's nothing like a crying baby throwing up on you to make you miss having someone else in the house to do clean-up duty. Then of course I got sick, too. So I was trying to take care of Emily, who was in the last days of her illness, while I was willing to sell my soul to stay in bed and feel sorry for myself just for a day. There's nothing like a baby to keep you from being lazy.

In the midst of the crying, puking, cleaning cycle, there was a knock on my door. The housing manager for our area stopped by to tell me I had to mow a patch of grass that had grown too tall—not the entire lawn, just one three-foot patch that was out of control. If I didn't "rectify the violation of housing regulations," I could be given a citation. As he told me this, I was holding Emily, secretly hoping she'd puke on him. She didn't.

"I'll take care of the grass as soon as I can. My husband is deployed, and my daughter is sick." OK, shameless play for sympathy. Hey, I have a friend who used the excuse of her husband being deployed to get out of a speeding ticket.

"See that it's done by next week when I do my next inspection." No sympathy at all. We didn't even own a lawn mower. When we first moved in, we had two neighborhood girls offer to cut our grass for ten dollars. I was perfectly happy with that arrangement. I had my hands full with Emily, and Paul despised yard work with unrivaled passion. (He had childhood memories of being forced to pull weeds as a punishment.) But when winter set in and the grass stopped growing, the girls disappeared, and I didn't know where to find them.

As the housing Nazi—I mean, *inspector*—started to walk away, I thought of another problem I was having at the house and stopped him.

"As long as you're here, can you tell me who I should call about my gutters?"

"What's wrong with them?"

I took him to the sidewalk and showed him the water that was stagnating in the gutter in front of my driveway. "The street is uneven so the water coming down just pools here. It's getting kind of gross."

He studied the brackish water for a moment and said, "Try raking it." Then he got in his car and drove away. That was when Emily threw up.

So now I had a sick baby, grass to mow and no lawn mower with which to accomplish that task, and gutters to rake. But wait, there's more—I was also working on our taxes.

We file our own taxes using a computer program. I was nearly done with the federal return when the program died, froze, crashed—call it whatever you want, I lost everything. Maybe there was a secret way to retrieve all the information, but there was no way I was going to try to find it. Paul is the computer geek in our house, and I have no problem playing damsel in distress when the computer doesn't do exactly what I want it to do. We both prefer it that way. So naturally I blamed Paul for the problem. If he'd been home, he could have fixed it and I wouldn't have had to start over again.

And just to be sure that I knew I was being singled out for aggravation, Murphy's Law threw me one more surprise. The lock on my mailbox chose that same week to break, and my mailman refused to deliver my mail until it was fixed. And of course I was hoping every day for a letter from Paul, which in and of itself was silly because my husband ranks letter writing just above yard work in his list of stuff he hates to do. But still, I checked the mail every day. So I put in a call to the maintenance office on base and had them come out to fix it. That took two days because they ended up having to rip the old lock out and install a new one. I pounced on my mail when it was finally delivered; no letter from Paul.

I spent the next three days in my yard during Emily's naptime. The first day I spent assembling the new lawn mower I bought. I will happily admit that I took some perverse pleasure in writing Paul (because *I* wrote *him* every day) that I had gone out shopping for a lawn mower.

It's just the kind of motorized, horsepower-driven, vaguely destructive tool that he loves to play with. Ha! If I have to mow, I get to pick it out. If Sears had had a pink one I probably would have bought it just out of spite. I proudly assembled it and even got the gas and oil filled up with a minimum of a mess. Of course the first time I started the thing I was convinced it was going to blow up. But in the end there was no giant fireball, and I cut down the offending patch of grass before the next inspection.

The next two days were spent—literally—raking water. I have never felt more ridiculous in my life. There I was, an intelligent, competent woman pushing water down a hill with a garden hoe. If you ever want to explore the depths of futility, I suggest trying to push puddles of water over a small bump in the road. After two days of clearing out the water and one very strong impulse to throw something at the guy up the street who decided to wash his car while I was raking my water farm, I had the gutters cleaned. My nerves were slightly frayed by the time I finished, and I stormed inside and composed my daily letter to Paul:

*Darling Paul,*

*I hate Saddam Hussein. I hate the Marine Corps. I hate grass. I hate gravity.*

*Love, Michelle*

The letter never made it to the mailbox (the lock hadn't been fixed yet, anyway) because Paul called later that night. I sobbed out the whole story, and in typical male fashion he picked out the one detail that interested him the most.

"So what kind of lawn mower did you get?"

He made me laugh. And that was the end of it.

The real problem behind the week from hell hadn't been the grass or the gutters or the mailbox. The problem was that I had felt alone. I didn't have my best friend, my partner there to help shoulder the burden and, yes, to mow the grass for me. The problem was that he was there and I was here and somehow I had to keep our life together while he was gone. It was all too much until he called and reminded me in his own way that he was still there for me and that we would get through this.

I told him the lawn mower was pink. And bless his heart, I think he believed me.

Eventually the lawn mower became a source of pride for me. Most of the Marines who lived on my street were also deployed to either Kuwait or Okinawa. I would go out every week with my Marine Corps cap on and mow my lawn with the mower I assembled myself. While out there I'd see the other wives mowing their lawns. We'd give that short "hi there" wave and go back to making our straight lines in the grass. I think we were all counting the days until we could pass the mowing duty back to our husbands. Jenny's husband was deployed, and she and I worked out an unspoken arrangement that we would alternate cutting the grass that grew in that no man's land space between our houses. I wasn't so lucky with my neighbor on the other side. He wasn't deployed, and he was a stickler when it came to exactly where he thought his lawn ended and mine began. It was just one big swatch of grass, but he would stop in the exact same place every week and never mow an inch more. One week when I did the mowing first I apparently stopped one pass too early. He mowed his lawn later that day and left one long streak of tall grass going right down the middle.

Just when I thought life was settling down, Murphy's Military Law tried one more time with me during the first two months of the deployment. One day as I climbed in the car with Emily to go to the commissary, my car refused to start. No *whirr, whirr,* no *sputter-sputter,* just *click.* Nothing. I had Paul's truck at the house, but it was a manual transmission and I couldn't drive a stick. (I never learned. OK, I refuse to learn; I drive automatics.) Paul got a great "I told you so" moment out of that.

Stranded at the house, I did call AAA this time and got a tow down to the garage on base. The diagnosis: my entire electrical system was shot. The mechanics said it looked like a rat had climbed into my engine and chewed through most of the wiring. I didn't freak out—I just laughed.

"So you're saying a rat ate my car? Yeah, that sounds about right."

# Chapter 6

# WAR

The first six weeks of the deployment were all about waiting. We knew deep down what was going to happen, it was just a question of when. The rest of the world may have been talking about diplomacy and peaceful solutions, but the wives back in Twentynine Palms knew with a strange kind of certainty that our men were going to war. But life had to go on while we waited.

The first few weeks following the deployment were chaotic. Because the unit had left in such a hurry, we were all taken by surprise, and the sudden loss of our husbands was a shock to the system. There hadn't been any time for preparation; it was literally here one day and gone the next for most of us. Jennifer's husband, Tony, had left on the same flight as Paul. Jennifer was expecting their first baby in June, and the day the news came down, Tony went with Jennifer to her doctor's appointment. They did an ultrasound and tried to determine the sex of the baby, but the little one wasn't cooperating. It was when Tony walked Jennifer out to her car after the appointment that he told her the news—the battalion was going to Iraq and he was leaving that night. Jennifer later told me that she should have known something was wrong when he walked her out to her car. She said he never did that after an appointment, he was always rushing back to work. Later that day when Paul and Tony were both at work trying to get everything ready to go, Jennifer came over to my house to go over the roster for H&S Company. We moved fast, each of us wanting to get it done so we could spend the rest of our day with our husbands. I took the communications platoon immediately because those were Paul's Marines. Jennifer took Tony's platoon, and we just blindly divided up the remainder of the roster. We wanted to make sure we had all the wives covered and that we had a consistent response for all the phone calls that would be coming in. Just as Paul and Tony were gearing themselves up for war, Jennifer and I were preparing for the war at home.

We planned to do a round of phone calls once the battalion left to make sure all of our wives knew how to get in touch with us if they needed to. I ended up with the CO's wife on my section of the roster. None of us knew her. She was an active-duty officer in the army, and she was based out in Virginia. Hmm, KVN training didn't cover the etiquette of this situation. I finally called her and left a message with my contact information. Then I followed it up with a short letter that had my name and phone number. Her name was on the roster, but it didn't have her rank. We all knew she was an officer, but no one knew anything else about her. Was she a major? A lieutenant colonel? I decided to err on the side of caution and addressed her as lieutenant colonel.

The following week, she called me and introduced herself. Turns out she was Major Kerry McCoy. Fortunately, she had a great sense of humor and didn't mind being promoted in my letter. We talked for a long time and stayed in touch throughout the deployment. Sometimes it was easy to forget that even though Kerry was an army officer and even though she was married to the CO, she was still in the same boat with the rest of us— a wife worried about her husband and hoping every day that he will come home.

The Key Volunteers started getting phone calls the day the first flight left. Many of the wives in the battalion were encountering problems. Though we had been trying to prepare ourselves for a possible deployment, a lot of the Marines in the unit still managed to leave their wives with some sort of problem. There were a number of quickie trips to Vegas (only three to four hours from the base, depending on how fast you drive) for instant marriages just before the deployment. Then when these new husbands left for Kuwait, their new wives were left behind with no clue as to what to do next. They needed ID cards, enrollment in Tricare (the military health-care system), applications for base housing—all of those important details that go much easier if the Marine is here to help navigate the military red tape. There were other wives who had never handled the family finances before and needed to know where to find their husband's pay information. It even got to the point where more than one wife asked me if I could get them their bank account and personal identification numbers. Most often though, we received calls from wives whose husbands had left them in some sort of lurch. One of my first calls was from a new wife whose husband owed the IRS a huge debt and hadn't told her about it. Now the IRS was calling her and demanding payment. This was actually the first "Can you help me?" phone call I received. The call went something like this.

"Hi, is this Michelle?"

"Yes it is. What can I do for you?"

"This is Danielle Spencer [not her real name]. My husband is in H&S Company, and he just left for Iraq and I have a huge problem."

"OK . . . " *Wow, there could be so many possible answers to this next question.* "What's going on?"

"We just got married a few months ago, and my husband owes the IRS like $7,000. The collection guy is calling me now, and he expects me to pay it."

"Well, that's not good. How can I help?"

"I need a few hundred dollars so I can call Roni Deutch and have her fix it."

*Time out.* I ask, "Who's Roni Deutch?"

"She's that tax attorney on TV. She says she can make tax debts go away for like twenty-five dollars. But I need to pay her first."

*Uhh . . . OK, let's think.*

"You know Danielle, we have attorneys here on base that won't charge you anything."

"Really?"

"Yes, the base legal office is located right across from the commissary. You should talk to them first."

"But do they do tax problems?"

"I don't know, but you should ask them. And if they say no you can always call Roni Deutch then." So I gave her the number, and when I called her back a few days later she was working with a military attorney who was helping get everything settled. Yeah for me—I answered the first question right! But it wouldn't be last one.

I don't know if money is actually the root of all evil, as the saying goes, but I do know it is the root of a lot of military family issues. I had a number of calls from wives who found out (usually on pay day) that their husbands had signed up for the split pay program, which allowed the Marines in Kuwait to withdraw money from their paycheck. This isn't a bad thing; most Marines did it. Problems occurred, however, when Marines sent most of their paycheck to the split pay program and didn't leave their wives enough to pay the bills. As Major Baker said, why do Marines need a thousand dollars a month in their pockets when they're sitting in the middle of the desert waiting for the green light to go into Iraq? Our guys were camped out in tiny green tents miles from civilization. It's not like they could run to McDonald's or Starbucks. Paul was drawing split pay, but he was taking out fifty dollars a paycheck and usually just sitting on it until someone had a chance to run to a permanent military base and buy him cigars. (My darling husband has two true weaknesses—Starbucks and cigars. My feeling on it was, the man is going into combat, so he should go ahead and have a latte and a cigar! Of course, if he had been drawing his entire paycheck in Kuwait for his cigar fund, I probably wouldn't have been so supportive.)

Other Marines hadn't left their wives with power of attorney (POA). Now this can be an interesting trust issue for

the Marines. It is recommended—highly recommended—
that Marines give their wives POA when they deploy so
their wives can act on their behalf while they're gone. Of
course, this means we can do *anything* with our husband's
finances, credit, and possessions. So for some husbands, it
becomes an "I trust you with my heart and my life, but not
my money" kind of situation. Paul has never thought
twice about it, and I've had POA for him the entire time
we've been married. (Every once in a while I remind
him that he's lucky I'm such a sweetheart.) Power of
attorney is necessary if a wife wants to apply for base
housing when her husband is gone, file taxes when he's
deployed (which was a very big deal since the battalion
would be gone for tax day), and buy or sell anything
with his name on it. (So I suppose if a wife was really
having a bad day during the deployment, she could sell
off her husband's prized sports car. But that's another
story, and I didn't do it!) We had quite a few frantic e-
mails and satellite phone calls going back and forth
between the rear party and the battalion in Kuwait
trying to get a number of POA arrangements done and
the split pay issues worked out before the unit crossed
over into Iraq.

As Key Volunteers, we helped when we could. Most
of the problems could be handled with a phone call to
the right base program. For the problems we couldn't
handle ourselves, we went to the rear party. We had two
staff sergeants in charge and a small group of enlisted
Marines; they were our official contacts with the

battalion. Of course with the satellite phones making the rounds in Kuwait and later Iraq, we were all getting calls from our husbands so we got unofficial information from them as well.

The rear-party Marines, like the KVs, were inundated with what I will call "what's going on?" calls. These calls were the most frequent. They were calls from a wife or mother or father or sister or grandmother of a Three-Four Marine who just wanted to know if anything had happened. Where was the battalion? What was going on? Had there been any casualties? We always explained that if and when the battalion moved or if something happened we would call all of the wives and let them know. But as the weeks dragged on, people started to get edgy and the calls increased.

I didn't mind the phone calls—except for one wife who always managed to call me at midnight. Not just once or twice, but every time she called me—midnight! Now if this had been two years before (in other words, before having a baby), I would probably have been awake and watching a movie at midnight. Nowadays though, at midnight I am in bed praying my daughter will sleep through the night. I knew these women were feeling the same uncertainty and anxiety that I was feeling. Answering their questions and easing their minds was what I had signed up to do. And calming down an upset wife helped calm me down too. When I spent most of the day telling wives that the Marines were fine, it made it easier for me to remember it too.

However, we encountered a problem when our phone numbers ended up on the Internet. One enterprising mother of a Three-Four Marine (who happened to be in Paul's platoon) developed a great website for family members of Three-Four Marines that became an amazing resource for families. But when she put the names and phone numbers of the Key Volunteers online, we suddenly found ourselves overwhelmed with phone calls. We were getting calls from people all across the country, and we had no way of knowing who they were, or if they were even really relatives of Three-Four Marines.

It's a terrible thing, but there was more than one scam going around during the war concerning phony casualty reports or Internet scams trying to get wives to give out their husband's personal information, resulting in identity theft. It sounds obvious that you shouldn't give out that kind of information over the phone, but for wives who were worried about their husbands, it was easy to get sucked in. Another base in California that had Marines in Iraq had a serious problem with wives receiving disturbing phone calls telling them their husbands had been injured or killed and that they needed to give the caller their husband's name and Social Security number to verify whether he was one of the injured Marines. When you get a call like that, it's pretty hard to keep your wits about you. How low does someone have to sink to steal from wives whose husbands have gone to war?

Though our phone numbers were removed from the website, we continued to receive phone calls from parents, aunts, and high school friends of deployed Marines throughout the deployment. It meant we had to be a lot more careful with the information we gave out over the phone. It could always be a reporter—or a terrorist. That sounds extreme, but it's not overreacting. At our information meeting with the wives, we made sure they knew not to believe anyone who called them on the phone with information about their husband being killed or injured. It could just be a tactic to hurt the morale of the troops and their families. And of course, our primary concern was always the safety of our Marines, so we didn't want anyone to give out information about their location over the phone. Every week the base newspaper reminded us, "Loose lips sink ships and get Marines killed. Don't discuss sensitive information over the phone."

In addition to fielding phone calls, the KVN also planned monthly social events for the families. It was far too easy during the deployment to hide away in your house, staring at the news all day and waiting for a phone call. It helped to have an outlet where everyone there knew what you were going through. Most of us experienced a strange disconnect from the rest of the world during the deployment. We lived in this vague limbo between the civilian world and the military one; we weren't active duty, but we weren't really civilians, either. I was fortunate to have an incredibly supportive circle of family and friends. But as much as their support meant to me (and it got me through some really bad days), there was still a huge gulf between their lives and mine.

"How *are* you, Michelle?" They'd ask with that sympathetic tone.

"I'm OK, thanks. How are you?"

"Oh, we're all fine. Have you heard from Paul?"

"Not recently, but I'm sure he's fine."

"Is there anything I can do?"

"No, I'm OK."

It wasn't that I didn't need help, it was that I just didn't know how to express it. I really didn't even know what I needed, aside from my husband coming home. I couldn't explain that I was lying awake at night staring into the darkness, wondering if my husband was alive. I couldn't explain that being the only one to care for my daughter day after day was slowly driving me insane. I knew the life I was living was so far removed from the rest of the world that I didn't even know how to describe it. So I didn't try.

"Wow, you're so strong," my friends would say. "I don't think I'd be able to keep it together like you if my husband was gone! How do you do it?"

*Ice cream and alcohol.* Just kidding, that's not true (OK, it's partly true).

I didn't know how I was doing it. There wasn't any special trick to it—this was just my life. I kept waking up day after day, taking care of Emily, writing Paul letters, and waiting. What other choice did I have? As Jennifer once said, "You get through it or you go crazy."

That's why the social events and my circle of friends within the battalion became so important. Maybe they weren't big, flashy events, just a picnic in the park or bowling, but when we all got together, we knew that everyone else there got it. Sure we spent plenty of time discussing the battalion's situation: Had they moved? Was mail finally getting through? Had they finally been able to take showers? Who had heard from her husband recently, and what did he say? But we were also able to tell each other when things weren't going well. We could look at each other and say, "This sucks," and everyone else would nod knowingly. We could complain and cry and sulk without fear of being judged or of giving the wrong impression to the civilian world. If our husbands were forging bonds in war that would last forever, back home we were creating a band of sisters with bonds that were just as strong.

That's not to say that it was all sisterhood and singing "Kumbaya." We had our share of personality conflicts and tensions. Some wives didn't deal with the deployment very well. They hid their worry in nasty attitudes and handled the stress and worry by complaining constantly. And because they had my name listed under "complaint department," I'd get calls that would make me cringe. Someone didn't like the rear party, base housing wasn't returning someone else's calls, someone's husband wasn't calling her enough—and what was I going to do about it? (Krista used to bug me to get caller ID so I could avoid the worst repeat offenders, but technology and I don't get along, so I never did.)

As Marine wives, especially those of us involved with the KVN, we were keenly aware of our responsibilities. While we might privately scream and rage against our husbands being sent halfway around the world, or we might complain to each other about being left behind, we would never say it to the media. It goes back to the love-hate relationship we had with them. We needed the information that the news broadcasts gave, but we also knew how damaging it could be to our Marines and the mood of the country in general to see Marine wives on television saying they resented the deployment. Lieutenant Colonel McCoy called it "shared courage." He was convinced that the wives staying strong back home had a direct impact on the ability of the Marines in the field to accomplish their mission. (That was one of the reasons he was such a big supporter of the KVN. The rumor was that when he came onboard as the new battalion CO, he told his staff, "Give the KVs whatever they want.") Our husbands had a job to do, and so did we. Maybe no one noticed what we were doing, but you can bet that if we had all suddenly showed up on the late-night news rallying against the war, it would have had a devastating impact. Maybe all we were doing was waiting and hoping, but it was enough.

Each company of volunteers rotated planning the monthly family events. Jennifer and I planned the event for March 2003. It was a simple family picnic at the base park we all called "the dinosaur park" because of the huge dinosaur slide. Jennifer was working off base and was also six months pregnant, so she asked me to do most of the initial paperwork for the picnic. The KVN had access to funds for use for family events but in order to get the money you had fill out all the right forms. It was my first time, but hey, I'm a capable woman, how hard could it be?

After pricing the items and filling out the purchase-order request form, I took it to Staff Sergeant Fabian Garcia in the rear party to have it signed.

"Fabian, could you sign this for me?"

"Sure, what is it?"

"A P.O. for food, drinks . . . ."

"What did you say?" Staff Sergeant Garcia asked, his eyes blinking like an owl.

"Food and drinks for the picnic next month."

"Oh, OK." He laughed and shook his head.

"What did you think I said?"

"I thought you said M–16s."

I laughed. "That's all we need. Let's arm the pissed-off wives of deployed Marines."

Staff Sergeant Garcia looked momentarily terrified. He, being in charge of the rear party, had dealt with more than his fair share of upset wives. "Let's not."

After getting his signature, I went over to the Marine Corps Community Services building to drop off the form for approval. The lady behind the desk (a civilian worker) was talking on the phone to her credit-card company. She talked and talked and talked and just signaled for me to wait. Now, I don't mind waiting, but Emily was sitting in her stroller and starting to get fidgety. When the lady finally finished scolding the person on the other end about the inaccuracies on her balance, she hung up and looked at me.

"Can I help you?"

"I just needed to drop off this form."

"What is it?"

"A P.O. for an upcoming Three-Four KV event." (See how the acronyms just infiltrate your vocabulary after a while.)

"Let me see it."

I passed it to her and waited while she pulled out a binder on her desk.

"This isn't the authorized signature," she said pointing to Staff Sergeant Garcia's name.

*Uh-oh.* "Who is the authorized signer?" I asked. I knew I had done exactly what Jennifer had told me to do.

Less-than-helpful Lady scanned her binder. "Lieutenant Colonel McCoy," she announced. "You'll need to have him sign this before I can process it."

I just stared at her for a second. "He's in Kuwait," I finally replied.

"Well, I can't process this without an authorized signature."

"But Staff Sergeant Garcia is our rear party OIC [officer in charge]."

"But he's not the authorized signer."

"Well, there isn't anyone else left. The battalion is deployed. How can we make him the authorized signer?"

"You'll have to have the commanding officer fill out a form authorizing Staff Sergeant Garcia to sign the purchase orders."

Ever feel like you're on a verbal merry-go-round?

"Our CO is Lieutenant Colonel McCoy," I said. She just looked at me. "He's *still* in Kuwait. I don't think he's planning on a trip back to sign a KV form."

"Well, I'm not sure I can help you."

Was it because I was the first person she saw after the credit-card issue? I ended up going back to Staff Sergeant Garcia and telling him the story. He was properly outraged and promised to take care of it. A few days later he called me and said I could pick up the money in about a week. I don't know what he said to Less-than-helpful Lady, but we didn't have further issues with our purchase orders. And as far as I know, Lieutenant Colonel McCoy never signed a single one.

On March 17, 2003, just a few days after the family picnic, President George W. Bush gave a speech to the nation. In it, he gave Saddam Hussein forty-eight hours to step down or risk military action. For the next two days the phone calls from Marine wives stopped almost entirely. We were all suddenly glued to our TVs, waiting for the announcement.

Paul called me the day after the president's speech. He sounded tense and somber.

"Do you know when you're going?" I asked him.

"Yeah, but I can't talk about it over the phone. I'm sure it will be on the news."

"How are you feeling? You sound tired."

"I'm OK. I'm just ready to get this thing going. The waiting has been hard on all of us."

"I know, us too. Are you worried?"

"No, we're going to destroy anyone who gets in our way." He was so filled with bravado and confidence that I almost forgot we were talking about a real war.

"How's Emily?"

"She's fine. She points at your picture whenever I change her diaper and says 'DaDa.' She's eating solid foods, although I freaked out the first time I gave her a cracker . . . I was just waiting for her to choke." There was silence for a long moment, and I felt bad for reminding Paul about everything he was missing. He would have laughed if he had seen me hovering over Emily with my finger ready to dial 911 at the first sign of that cracker not going down. He would have liked that day.

"She must be getting so big," he said softly.

"She is. I love you, Marine."

"I love you too. I don't know if I'll be able to call again once we cross the LD [line of departure] into Iraq. So don't worry if you don't hear from me."

"I'm always going to worry."

"I know. I'm sorry."

And I knew right then that part of him was sorry he was doing this to me. He was sorry he was putting his family through this. And just as he didn't want me to worry about him, I didn't want him worrying about me when he was going into harm's way. So even though my throat was tightening and I could feel tears burning my eyes, I tried to keep everything light.

"There's no place I'd rather be. Hey, tell Tony to call Jennifer."

It was customary for Paul and me to pass messages along in our phone calls. More than once he asked me to call a wife and tell her that her husband was doing a great job. And just as often, I told him to go find a Marine and tell him to call home, his wife was worried. In one oft-repeated story, I told Paul to go find our friend Steve and have him call Justine. She hadn't heard from him in weeks, and she was quickly going from worried to freaked out to just plain pissed off. Paul found Steve, who was with an artillery battery.

"Captain Pritchard, do you have a minute?" Steve outranked Paul, but once they were alone the formality dropped. "Dude, call your wife—now," Paul said. And Steve did.

A number of times, wives of Marines in Paul's platoon would call me to pass along concerns about their husbands. Most of the time their husbands had written home with complaints, and the wives would call me thinking I could talk to Paul on their husband's behalf. I called it the wives' grapevine. I didn't mind passing the information along to Paul, and I'm sure more than once the tactic backfired for the Marine. But sometimes Paul learned about issues he might not have heard about other-wise. After the last time Paul called before the battalion moved into Iraq, we were all on edge. It wasn't long before we got the call. In my case, Jennifer called me. "They're on the move. They're in Iraq."

And suddenly everything changed.

The information about the Marines going into Iraq had filtered down from the rear party who had contacted Ann, the Key Volunteer advisor, and Krista, the coordi-nator. Ann and Krista then told the company coordinators, who then told the company volunteers. Then we all called the wives on our list. The conversations I had with the wives I called were strikingly similar.

"Hi, this is Michelle, your Key Volunteer. I'm calling to let you know that the battalion has crossed into Iraq, and they're on the move."

"Where are they?"

"We don't have that information right now. All we know is that they have moved into Iraq."

This was the official information. As representatives of the command, the Key Volunteers had to be very careful to only give out official information. Unofficially, though, we were all comparing notes. The group of lieutenants' wives would pass along any information we had gleaned from conversations with our husbands and try to piece it all together like a jigsaw puzzle. For security reasons, Marines were not supposed to give out any information about where they were going, and we all understood that. But if, say, Paul told me they were going to head north, and Tony told Jennifer they were heading to a town starting with B, and if Frank told Stephanie they were located to the west of the army position—pretty soon we had them plotted on a map.

By this time, each of us had our favorite news channel. Fox News was my constant companion. We also had John Koopman. John was a reporter for the *San Francisco Chronicle,* embedded with Three-Four. He was writing articles on the battalion, and we wives were devouring them. Generally one of us would see a new article online and send out a massive e-mail with a link. We loved the articles because they told us more than we were getting from the rear party. When Three-Four began to see combat, those articles became a mixed blessing. We wanted to know what was going on, we were desperate for even the smallest details, but at the same time none of us wanted to read about the attacks, the danger, the deaths.

There was never enough information. The news was covering the war twenty-four hours a day, but it wasn't specific enough for us. The news would broadcast casualties, and we would watch for agonizing hours trying to get information. Was it army or Marine? (We all began to rail against the reporters who used the word "soldiers" as a generic descriptor. The army has soldiers—the Marines have Marines.) If they reported that a Marine had been killed, we waited for them to give us a base. Was he from Twentynine Palms? What unit was he with? Tell us more. Was it my husband? But all we could do was wait.

# Chapter 7

# THE KNOCK ON THE DOOR

About forty-eight hours after the president's ultimatum on March 17, 2003, we began to see bombs over Baghdad. The president addressed the nation again with assurances of victory, but also warnings of casualties. I knew, logically, that in war not everyone comes home. I thought of it when I said good-bye to Paul that morning in January. I looked around at the Marines standing in their uniforms ready to go to war, some of them only eighteen or nineteen years old, some older with wives and children, and I wondered, was I casually looking at a man who wouldn't make it back? That's the ugly truth of combat: people die.

But listening to the president talk about the potential for U.S. casualties, I was struck by a bizarre sense that he was describing the most morbid lottery ever devised. My husband, my friends were over there—all potential casualties. Who would it be? Who was going to become a statistic? I was praying every night that it wouldn't be Paul. I wanted him to come home; I wanted him to see Emily grow up, to walk her down the aisle at her wedding. But if Paul was going to come home, who wouldn't make it?

At one of the first KVN meetings after the Marines had deployed in January, one of the questions we all wanted answered was: What will happen if my husband is killed? It was a sort-of defense mechanism. We wanted the information, to know down to the smallest detail what to expect if the worst should happen.

It would all begin with a knock on the door, we were told. Notification times were between 6 a.m. and 10 p.m.

A Marine, usually one of the rear party, would arrive at our door in his dress blue uniform and tell one of us that our husband would never come home again.

I think most of us got to the point where we hated to have someone stop by unannounced. Once the Marines moved into Iraq, my friend Justine and I agreed to call one another before we came over just so there wouldn't be an unexpected knock on the door. For me, it never failed. Every time someone rang my doorbell or knocked, my heart would skip a beat, and I'd find myself praying, "Please God no, please God no," as I walked to the door. It's a terrifying way to live, afraid to open your own door because of what might be waiting for you. Jennifer summed it up best one day when she said, "Anytime there's a Marine in his dress blues at your front door and it's not the Marine Corps ball, it's bad news."

From what I could tell, the wives were split into two camps when it came to the knock-on-the-door nightmare. Half of them refused to think about it, refused to even spend one minute thinking about what would happen if their husband were killed. The other half deliberately spent time imagining it, trying to decide how they would react, what they would do, whom they would call. I fell into the latter category. I made a plan— just in case.

I always wanted Paul to come home. I can't say I always believed he would. I can remember very clearly one night when I was taking a shower, and it suddenly hit with violent force that Paul could be killed. It wasn't just the normal, logical understanding that he was in a dangerous situation and death was a possibility. No, this night I was just gripped with a certainty that he was going to die—and there was nothing I could do to stop it. I wouldn't even be able to say good-bye to him. I stood in the shower sobbing until the water turned cold.

Maybe it was morbid, maybe it was superstitious, but I thought about getting the knock on the door. I planned what I was going to do if it ever came. My first priority was to stay calm. I didn't want to collapse on the floor; I didn't want to scream. I imagined over and over going to the door, seeing the Marine in his dress blues and just knowing; before he would even say a word, I would know. I would invite him in; we'd sit in the family room. I always hoped that if the news ever came, my mom or dad would be visiting so they could take Emily into another room while I heard the news. Even though she was only a baby I didn't want her there when a Marine told me her daddy was dead.

If I was alone when this happened, I knew my first call would be to Jennifer. We had been told that the casualty-notification Marines wouldn't leave a wife home alone after she'd been given the news. They had to wait until someone else was with her. Well, Jennifer and I were of similar mindsets that if our husbands were killed, we'd need some time alone to process the information. So she and I agreed that if the time ever came for either one of us, we'd call the other to come over just long enough for the Marine to leave, and then we'd leave the other alone.

I imagined that after I called Jennifer and the Marine had gone, I'd call my mom. But, being a flight attendant, she might be out of the country, so I would need to call her supervisor at United Airlines. I made sure I knew where that number was. Then I'd call my dad. He'd probably be on the next flight down. I knew Paul's mom was on his emergency-notification form, so the Marines would personally inform her. But I'd have to call her and Paul's sister. I imagined that I'd probably send an e-mail letting all of our friends know what had happened. That sounds so impersonal, but I couldn't imagine having to have that conversation again and again and again.

Paul and I had already talked about what he wanted, so I knew I'd have to call the church in San Diego where we were married. I had a horrible vision of sitting in the front pew at Paul's funeral not even three years after we had been married there. Then there would be a graveside service with the military honors. I knew Paul wanted to be cremated and his ashes scattered in the sea. But should I wait to scatter them until Emily was old enough to understand? Would it matter to her?

When we were still stationed at Quantico, Paul had been volunteered to be an honor attendant at the Makin Raiders funeral. It was the burial of the remains of fourteen Marines who had been killed during World War II, and whose bodies had only recently been found and identified. Paul was honored and so nervous about it. He was going to be presenting the flag to one of the family members. He wanted to do it right, and he asked to practice on me. He took the tri-folded flag, knelt before me, and said the words I never wanted to hear:

"On behalf of the President of the United States, the United States Marine Corps, and a grateful nation . . ."

*No, no, no! I won't listen!*

I wish I could say that I couldn't imagine my life without Paul, but I imagined it far too often. We were living in base housing, so I knew we'd have six months before we'd have to move out. Where would we go? My mom lived in Palm Springs, so Emily and I could get a house down there. My dad and stepmother lived in northern California in the house I grew up in, so we could move up there. We'd need our own place, but I'd have to find a job. I could teach, or maybe I should go back to law school. How would I support Emily on my own?

Those were the thoughts that kept me up at night. Was Paul hurt? Was he suffering? What if he was captured? Over and over—nightmares that wouldn't stay in the dark, but would pop out at me unexpectedly during the day. What was Paul doing right now? Was he alive? Was he hurt? Was there a Marine on his way to my house right now?

Then somehow Paul would manage a phone call, even if it was only for a few minutes, and I'd know he was OK. For those few minutes that we could talk, I'd know he was alive and unhurt. Maybe he hadn't showered in weeks or had a decent meal in days, but he was alive; those conversations were the only times I was absolutely certain of it. The rest of the time, I was living on faith.

Not long after the beginning of the war, there were Marine casualties. I remember the news reported that there were six Marines killed: four had been killed in a helicopter crash and two others in ground fighting. That was a bad day. I kept telling myself Paul was fine. Why would he be in a helicopter? That didn't make any sense. But what about the other two—the news didn't report where they were from or what unit they were with. But it couldn't be Paul. I would know if something had happened to him, right? Certainly some deep cosmic feeling or some premonition would prepare me for the news. But what if I were going through my normal day, playing with Emily, cooking dinner, and paying bills not even knowing that my husband was already dead? Could it really happen like that?

When the news of the first Marine deaths hit, I received a ton of phone calls. Not only from Three-Four wives who were worried, but also from my friends and family. I remember a conversation with one of my best friends, Caty. She was so good about calling me to see how I was doing. She was one who would have understood if I burst into tears on the phone. I think the fact that I never did burst into tears worried her more.

"Michelle, I just heard about the Marines who were killed. Is Paul OK?"

"I don't know. I haven't heard from him since they crossed into Iraq."

"Do you know if he was in the area? I mean, he's fine, right?"

"As far as I know. No one's come to my door to tell me otherwise. And until they do, I'm going on faith that he's OK."

There was silence on the other end of the phone. The kind where your friend just dropped a bombshell, and you want to say something, but nothing seems to fit. "God, Michelle, is that what it's like? Just waiting for bad news? How do you do it?"

Now, I said Caty wouldn't care if I spilled my sorrows to her. In fact she'd be the best one to go to, but I never did. My job was to stay strong and stay positive.

"It sounds worse than it is . . . really." *Liar, liar, pants on fire.*

As we would find out the next day, no one from Three-Four had been hurt.

It was a few weeks after the war had started when Three-Four had its first death. Lance Corporal Mark Evnin was killed in a firefight following an ambush. For us back home, word came slowly. The first I heard of it was when one of my wives in H&S Company called me.

"I heard a Three-Four Marine was killed. Is it true?"

Ironically, I called these types of calls "ambush calls." They were those when a wife called me with information I hadn't received from the command yet, and they frustrated me to no end. Fortunately, I had a standard response to this type of question.

"We don't have any official word on that yet."

"But who was it?"

"Nothing has been released yet, so I don't have any

information I can tell you. They won't release his name until his family has been notified."

"But what if it's my husband?"

*What if it's mine?*

"Honestly, you would know that before I did. Remember, no news is good news. So as long as no one has come to your door, your husband is fine."

After I got off the phone, I immediately called Jennifer. She'd heard there had been a death, but didn't know who or even what company he belonged to. For that entire day we all waited. My phone rang constantly. Did I know anything yet? It took three days for us to finally get the official word. By then, though, the news media had already covered it, and everyone knew. As KVs, we were frustrated that the chain of information had broken down and that we had been unable to answer questions from the wives. As wives, we were at once relieved that our Marine was still alive, and at the same time we were made painfully aware that our guys weren't sitting on the sidelines. They were in the middle of it.

The command tried to fix the way information was passed about casualties after Evnin's death. When the battalion lost another Marine a few weeks later, I got a call from Paul.

"We lost another Marine," he said bluntly. He gave me the information on it and then said "Major Baker wants you to call Ann and make sure she knows what's going on. He tried to call her already, but she didn't answer her phone."

Hmm—difficult moment. "Paul, I can't pass 'unofficial' information."

Not long before this phone call, I had spoken with Ann, and she told me to be very careful with the information I passed to my wives. We were not supposed to pass along any information that was not given to us officially by the command. We had just recently been yelled at for telling the wives that mail had finally gotten through to the unit. The information had come from satellite phone calls and hadn't been "officially passed" yet. So, I was really worried about the reaction of passing information about casualties. It wasn't just a fear of getting yelled at again, but a fear of what would happen to Paul. Technically speaking, a wife can't do anything to impact her husband's career. The command is supposed to ignore everything that wives do and not hold it against the Marines. But it still made me nervous.

"Honey, his family has already been notified," Paul said. "Just tell Ann to check in with the rear party."

So I called Ann, and we got the official word. This time we were prepared for the phone calls, but it didn't make it any easier knowing that another Marine wasn't coming home.

## Chapter 8

# CARE PACKAGES
# AND
# COUNTRY MUSIC

My mother, being a flight attendant, can pack her entire life into one piece of carry-on luggage. This is a skill she has passed on to me, and it comes in really handy for vacations and road trips. Turns out it also comes in handy when your husband goes to war. During the months Paul was deployed, I elevated the humble care package into a work of packing art. And I got plenty of practice.

I tried to send off a package to Paul every other week. Some were big, some small, but they were always full. It was all very scientific, and it got to the point where I didn't even need packing peanuts or newspaper to cushion the goodies anymore.

Of course, it took some practice, and the first care package was a learning moment. I had a huge box, and it was stuffed with all sorts of goodies. My mom had suggested that I use newspaper to cushion everything so when Paul unpacked it, he could read the paper. She said that was one of the things she had done when she had made care packages for friends during Vietnam. So I did. Then I made my first fatal mistake. I sent homemade cookies. Well, this was back during the beginning of the deployment, when the mail system was still all goofed up, and Paul didn't even get the box for six weeks. By then the cookies had turned into building materials, and he never even looked at the newspaper. Turns out that small packages seemed to make it to the guys faster than really big boxes.

Every time I went to the commissary or Wal-Mart, I would pick up things Paul needed, or more often than not, things I thought he needed or might like. It wasn't easy at first. What do you send a guy who's camped out in the middle of the Kuwaiti desert preparing to go to combat? Then what do you send once he goes into combat?

The answer: baby wipes.

In the desert, baby wipes were like gold. Showers were few and far between, so often times baby wipes were the only things the Marines had to clean up with. So whenever I picked up a package of wipes for Emily, I grabbed an extra pack for Paul. I had an entire section of counter space in my kitchen dedicated to care package supplies: baby wipes, cookies, lotion, sunscreen, Q-Tips, coffee, Gatorade powder, Tang, lemonade (anything to cover the taste of the water they were drinking), pens, cards, candy, underwear, socks, pictures of Emily. Then I'd get a box and stuff it full of whatever would fit. Paul laughed when he told me he never knew what to expect when he opened a package from me. It wouldn't be odd for him to find a box of Oreos, some batteries, instant noodles, and a video game sitting on top of a bag with sunscreen, a razor, and toothpaste and to have everything cushioned with green socks. And always, baby wipes.

Of course, I wasn't the only one sending Paul packages. My aunt became the toilet-paper fairy. She would send him boxes filled with nothing but toilet paper. And because Paul had to be able to carry everything with him when they were on the move, he didn't have a lot of extra space. So my aunt would buy rolls of Charmin (Paul's favorite), unroll the entire roll, remove the cardboard center, then re-roll all the toilet paper back into a tiny roll. She was really happy when I told her she could buy toilet paper rolls without the cardboard tube (Wal-Mart, camping section).

And Paul did really well for himself during Girl Scout cookie season. I bought thirty boxes myself (yes, you read that correctly—thirty boxes) and rationed them out over a few months of care packages. My dad and stepmother also bought Girl Scout cookies for Paul and sent him twenty boxes all at once. When sending cookies, the only problem we had to deal with was the heat. Even though it was only March, Iraq was already warming up and anything chocolate would melt. Sometimes it took up to a month for packages to reach the Marines; that's a lot of time for cookies to sit in the heat. But most of the Marines would tell us later that melted cookies were still a few steps above their MREs (Meals, Ready-to-Eat).

Care packages became a ritual. It wasn't just me—most of the wives were regularly sending off boxes of goodies. We all got to know the guys working in the base post office really well. And we became pros at filling out the international customs forms. Care packages were always a topic of conversation when we got together. Did anyone have any ideas for something new to send? What did the guys need?

Of course, being in the military, there were rules regarding care packages. I like to call it the "no porn, pork, or alcohol" rule. Because the Marines were in a Muslim country, they were expected to respect the local culture as much as possible. This meant no pornography. At the KVN information meetings when we announced the care package rules to the wives, the "please don't send your husband pornography" part of the evening was pretty fun. Then we had to explain that it wasn't just *Playboy* and *Penthouse*. Even *Maxim* and the *Sports Illustrated* swimsuit edition were off limits. And we weren't to send naked pictures of ourselves. I don't know how many wives actually followed these rules, but I do know that in spite of the rule, there was never a shortage of "male entertainment" in the desert.

At this same meeting we also explained that we couldn't send pork products. This was again because of Muslim culture. I remember quite distinctly one wife who was outraged that she couldn't send her husband pork rinds. He loved his pork rinds. Why couldn't he enjoy his fried pig snacks? After all, he wasn't Muslim. There was no calming her down, and she swore that if her husband were going into combat he'd be going with pork rinds. Kind of hard to argue with that kind of devotion.

There were also common-sense rules to follow. No firearms or ammunition. (Yeah, I think the guys were pretty set with stuff that blows up.) No tobacco in excess of 100 grams. (I knew of wives who were buying chewing tobacco by the case and sending it over.) And finally, no alcohol. (I heard second- or thirdhand about one wife who bought bottled water, emptied the bottles and refilled them with vodka then glued the caps back on. Got to admire the creativity.)

For me, I never sent secret caches of vodka or tubs of tobacco. Paul likes his cigars but he could find better ones there than I could get back home. And I didn't send naked pictures of me or anyone else. Paul said he wouldn't have minded if had broken that rule, but I didn't like the idea of pictures of me in my birthday suit floating around an infantry battalion.

For months during my shopping trips to the commissary with Emily sitting in the cart, I would wonder out loud, "What else should we send Daddy?" If there was another wife passing by during one of my chats with my nine-month-old daughter, she might stop and offer a suggestion, something her husband had requested or had really liked. I tried to imagine what would make life easier for Paul, what would make him smile, or what he was missing. On one shopping trip, I found myself standing in the coffee aisle staring at the instant creams. Paul loves coffee, but can't stand to drink it black. He pours enough cream in his coffee to turn it from black to very pale beige.

"Why don't you just drink water?" I always teased him.

"I like coffee."

"That's not coffee, that's coffee-flavored milk."

Standing in front of the assorted powered creamers, I started crying. Not big sobs, but little tears that just appeared out of nowhere. It suddenly became vitally important that I know if Paul was able to put cream in his coffee. I was absolutely certain there was coffee in the camp—in every war movie, there's always coffee. But is there cream?

I have no idea how long I stood there, but I bought five bottles of powdered cream that day.

Later, when I told Jennifer about my commissary breakdown she nodded knowingly. Every one of us had it at least once: that moment in the commissary or grocery store where you pick up something your husband loves, something you always bought to have on hand in the house, then you suddenly realized that he wasn't going to be home to enjoy it. Or a time when the very act of picking up baby wipes or beef jerky to send to Iraq was immediately overwhelming, a symbol of everything that was out of control and uncertain in your life. As much as I felt terrible when one of my friends would have one of these bad moments, it always made me feel a little less crazy to know I wasn't the only one who cried over cream or spinach.

The funny thing (or sad thing depending on whether or not your husband is deployed) is that as much as I refused to break down in front of my friends or family, as much as I worked at keeping up a strong front, the stupidest things would get to me—like crying in the powdered cream aisle. I may have been able to pull off the "I'm fine, don't worry about me" line with friends, but when I was alone or if it was just Emily and me, I was Niagara Falls just waiting to happen.

I've always had a soft spot for music; while the news broadcasts and phone calls from friends didn't get to me like they did for some wives, music was my Achilles heel. Country music got to me all the time. You'd think after the first two months I'd have gone back to good old-fashioned rock and roll, but no, I was a glutton for emotional punishment. There was a Lonestar song out at the time called "I'm Already There." It ended up being something of an anthem for military wives everywhere. I only needed to hear the first line, and I was a mess of tears and tissues. There were many other songs about the war that started to come out, and I was pretty much a goner whenever I turned on the car radio. And if "God Bless the U.S.A." hit the airwaves while I was driving, I had to pull over or risk plowing into a sand dune. And any song about love, loneliness, or loss would send me over the edge.

All of the wives had something different that would hit us and bring the reality of our lives crashing back in on us. We could go for days, living our life as normally as possible, knowing that our husband was in harm's way, but not dwelling on it—then *wham!* Something happened, and it all hit home, again and again and again. Maybe it was a song or a movie or just driving by his favorite restaurant. Maybe it was finding one of his socks that had fallen behind the hamper before he left or finally getting a letter from him.

We lived in this cycle of almost believing we had a normal life, getting through the days just fine, then suddenly there was the "Oh my God, I can't do this" moment. We'd cry or scream, break something, or binge on chocolate, and it would pass. Then we'd go back to getting through each day. When I'd catch myself doing something normal, I'd think, *How can I be sitting here calmly reading a book or playing with Emily or doing my makeup when my husband is in a war zone?* It just really came down to realizing that there was nothing else I could do.

I'm a fairly huge control freak. (Or, as one of my Marine friends—don't worry, you'll meet him in the second deployment—said once, "I'm not a control freak, I just want things done my way.") So accepting the fact that there was nothing more I could do during the deployment except wait and hope was a big deal for me. I was writing Paul every day, I was sending two or three care packages a month, I had my volunteer work with the battalion, and I was raising Emily; that was all I could do. I couldn't make the war go faster, I couldn't bring Paul home. The situation was completely out of my hands, and all I could do was get through it. That's not to say I didn't have my bad days, I had plenty of them, we all did. But what else could I do? When people would ask me "how do you do it?" there was only one response: I don't have a choice. I could pack it in, send Paul a "Dear John" letter—"Dear Paul, Thanks for the good times, but this is too much, I'm outta here." Or I could stay, stick it out, and pray that he'd come home soon.

I stayed. And I stayed because I loved him and that was enough.

I compulsively checked my e-mail two or three times a day. Though Paul wasn't e-mailing me, I kept hoping that one day he would——he's much better at typing an e-mail than writing a letter. Or there might be an update from the KVN or a new article from John Koopman. So I kept checking: in the morning when Emily was watching *The Wiggles*, in the afternoon during her nap, and then at night once she went to bed. On the morning of April 4, 2003, I was still in my robe when I fired up the computer.

Jessica Wessman, the KV who had reintroduced me to the joys of high heels had sent me an e-mail. It was short and simple.

*Dear Michelle.*

*I didn't know if you had seen this yet, but thought I'd send it to you just in case.*

*Jessica.*

There was an attachment, so I opened it. And there was Paul. He wearing his flak jacket and helmet and holding a small Iraqi girl in his arms. He was smiling down at her as she looked into the camera.

I had no idea what to think. I was so happy to see him, to see that he was safe and healthy. But I didn't know what I was looking at. What had happened? Who was the little girl? Where was the picture taken?

I didn't have to wait long. Pretty soon I was flooded with e-mails from people who had seen the photo online and were sending it to me. Eventually Paul was able to call. He explained that the girl had been wounded when her parents had driven a car through a Marine checkpoint. The Marines had fired on the car, and her parents had been killed. Paul had taken her to the doctors for medical attention. (Months later, after Paul had come home, he wondered what had happened to her. He knew where she had been taken for treatment, but not what happened later.)

Over the next few days, the photo of Paul and the girl was everywhere. I found it in a couple of different newspapers. In one San Diego paper, it appeared just below another picture of Three-Four Marines in the middle of a battle to secure a key bridge into Baghdad. After that I saw the photo in a montage that aired on the Fox News Channel during *The O'Reilly Factor*. It was on for weeks, and every night after it aired, I'd get phone calls. "Did you see Paul on TV?" I watched Bill O'Reilly anyway, but I found myself watching for the Iraq War photos just to get a glimpse of Paul's picture. Unless Paul had actually called, seeing that photo was usually the best three seconds of my day.

Most of my friends called within a few days of Paul's picture hitting the papers and news shows. My "almost" mother-in-law, the mom of my bodybuilder-turned-priest ex-boyfriend, cut out five copies of the picture and had them laminated. Emily loved to carry those pictures around with her. I always liked it when someone called about the photo. It seemed like it made the war more personal to people outside of my strange military world. I knew that whenever someone saw the photo, they'd say, "Hey, there's Paul," and they'd think of him. And some-times they'd think of me, too, and call to check in.

During the deployment, a few college friends who lived in Los Angeles drove out to the base for visits. My best friend (also named Michelle) drove out with her husband and their son, Tyler, who was six months younger than Emily. Jeff, Michelle's husband, joked that when Paul came back from Iraq he was going to bring camels and goats to use as Emily's dowry when we formally arranged a marriage between Emily and Tyler. It was a good visit, and it meant a lot to me that they'd made the nearly four-hour drive complete with baby boy. Michelle wanted to know when Emily and I were going to leave the glamour of the base and stay with them for a few days.

I had the same offer from another college friend. Rob drove out for a brief visit and asked if I wanted to spend some time at his new house with his wife and their two kids. And of course my dad and stepmother wanted us to camp out in northern California for as long as possible.

I turned down every offer. Not because I didn't want the company or need the break—I'm still amazed I didn't end up running wild through the streets after being a single mom to an infant for so long—but I couldn't leave the base. I wasn't held hostage, there were no bars on my windows, and the guards wouldn't have given it a second thought if I had packed up everything in a U-Haul and split. But I needed to stay.

I had a reasonable excuse in my KVN work; I really did have an obligation to my wives. I was on the phone every day and helping organize events. But more than that, I needed to be in our house. Paul was still there—in the pictures, the books, his clothes, his uniforms. I needed to be in our bed, the bed we bought when we first moved in together back in San Diego. That was our home, and I couldn't stand the thought of it being empty.

But if I'm going to be brutally honest, there was another reason I didn't indulge in a week or two away: fear.

What if I was visiting Michelle and something happened to Paul? How would the Marines find me? What if they gave up on trying to locate me and released the information on the news? I didn't want to find out that way. I knew logically I could have simply notified the rear party, let them know where I would be and how to reach me. I was constantly reminding my wives to let us know if they leave the area so we could reach them if we needed to. But I just couldn't do it. Maybe I talked myself into being superstitious, or maybe it was just good old fashioned fear, but I couldn't bring myself to leave the base.

# Chapter 9

# THE DAY THE STATUE FELL

During the deployment I had plenty of bad days and a few good days. April 9, 2003, was a good one. It started out just like every other day. I woke up, took Emily out of her crib, made breakfast, turned on the news, and lo and behold, what do I see? Marines in Baghdad.

I watched, transfixed, like most of the world, as Marines and soldiers rolled into the city. There were cheering Iraqis and even whispers of smiles on the faces of some of the servicemen. Was this the end? Was it over? We're in Baghdad; Saddam has fled! Is this the day?

Then something truly amazing happened. As I sat watching the live coverage of Iraqis chipping away at a huge statue of Saddam Hussein, a tank retrieval vehicle rolled into the square. I thought it was just going to knock the statue down, but it stopped. I'm sure most of us remember that moment, watching the Marines (and I knew they were Marines because they were wearing the new digital-pattern camouflage uniforms that no other branch of the service had) attach a rope to the head of Saddam and then yank that statue down. It was a movie moment: the crescendo of music, the heroes topple the villain and then—the end. It didn't take long once that statue fell for me to begin to wonder, *When are they coming home?*

Jennifer called me just minutes after it happened. "Did you see it?"

"Yes. Can you believe it?"

"It feels like it's over, doesn't it?"

"It does. We've won." Then there was a pause, and we

both thought the same thing: "So when do you think they can come home?"

Now by this time Jennifer was seven months pregnant. She was due in June, and we were all hoping that Tony would make it back in time for the birth. Jennifer was ready to go through it alone, though. I asked her once if she had thought about asking someone else to be her labor coach.

"No," she replied. "If Tony's not here, I'll do it myself." They say it takes a special kind of man to be a Marine. Well, I think it takes a special kind of woman to marry one.

Watching the Marines in Baghdad, though, suddenly made it seem like the deployment could come to an end quicker than any of us had thought.

Not long after I talked to Jennifer, my phone rang again. It made a good day even better.

"Hello?"

"Hey, honey."

"Paul? Oh my God, where are you?"

"Baghdad. It's been crazy."

"I know, I've been watching the news all morning. I saw a group of Marines pull down a huge statue of Saddam Hussein."

"You did? That was us."

"You? What do you mean?"

"That was us, Three-Four. We pulled it down. I was there."

My husband has some talent for finding the media. "Where were you?"

"Standing at the front of the vehicle. Up on the right."

"I'm going to look for you the next time they show the footage. I can't believe what's happened. It's amazing."

"I was just interviewed for the *Today Show*."

"Really. That's so cool."

"Yeah, but I forgot to say hi to you and Emily. Sorry."

"That's OK. I didn't hear it anyway."

"I also met [TV news correspondent] Christiane Amanpour. She's incredible. She autographed one of the pictures I have of me and Emily."

"So does this mean its over? We won and we're done?"

Paul paused. "Not yet."

I heard a series of pops in the background.

"What was that? Was that gunfire?"

"Yeah. But don't worry, if they shoot me, it's probably a mistake."

"That doesn't make me feel better."

"It's the same fight, honey. Just a different location."

"So you don't know if you guys are coming home anytime soon?"

"I don't think so. I'm sorry. We've still got a lot of work to do."

"Oh."

"But we're closer to home now than we were a month ago."

"I know. I just don't want you guys to get stuck over there—like policemen."

"That probably won't happen. I don't know how long it will be, but I think the worst is over."

"OK."

"I love you."

"I love you too. I miss you, Marine."

"I miss you too. Can I talk to Emily?"

I held the phone to Emily's ear as I often did when Paul called. She'd listen, and I think she recognized his voice. Sometimes her eyes would widen, and she'd pull back to stare at the phone like she couldn't figure out how her daddy squeezed into that tiny space. When she'd start squirming, I'd take the phone back.

"She's been chewing on your picture. I think that means she loves you." There's a long silence on the other end.

"I miss you both so much."

"I know. We miss you too. Hey?"

"Yeah?"

"I'm proud of you."

"Thanks, honey. I gotta go. There are more Marines who want to call home. If you talk to any comm wives tell them all their men are fine." He knows I'm not supposed to tell the wives that kind of "unofficial" information, but he tells me anyway and I pass it along anyway. "I love you. Kiss Emily for me and tell her Daddy loves her."

"I will. I love you too. Stay safe, Marine."

My phone rang constantly that day. Wives, friends, family—everyone was ecstatic. It was over. We had won. Saddam Hussein was gone, there hadn't been any chemical weapons used, and most of the Marines in Three-Four had safely made it to Baghdad. Now the question on everybody's mind was: *How soon can they come home?*

When the unit deployed, we had been told to prepare for the men to be gone a year. But it had only been two and a half months, and they were already in Baghdad. I tried not to get my hopes up. I knew there was still a chance that they could stay there to help keep the peace, provide security, and restore law and order. There was just no way of knowing. I had a number of wives call me over the following week, wanting information. Most of them had heard from their husbands, and every Marine who called home had a different opinion on when they were coming home.

I know people like to make fun of women for being gossips, and as Marine wives we have taken our fair share of teasing for the speed of our wives' grapevine. But I can tell you with absolute authority, there are no bigger gossips in the world than Marines in a combat zone. We called it the rumor mill, and we could barely keep up with all the misinformation that began flying between wives. I started to dread answering my phone.

"Hello?" *Please let it be a telemarketer.*

"Hi, Michelle. It's Jane." (Made-up name, true conversation.) "Is it true the guys are coming home next week?"

*Uhhh . . . OK. I'll play.* "We haven't had any word on that, but I don't think it's possible for them to get out that quickly."

"But I just talked to Susie"—*I think I know Susie*—"who heard from Jill"—*who's Jill?*—"that her husband called her and told her that he heard from one of the guys that they were getting ready to come home. I said I'd call you because you're the Key Volunteer. So, is it true?"

My eyes were crossing. "Listen Jane, there are a bunch of rumors circulating right now about when the unit will be coming back. What I can tell you for sure is that there hasn't been any official word from the command on it. As far as I know there aren't any plans set for bringing them home." I hate being the bearer of bad news.

"But Jill's husband heard it."

"He probably overheard some speculation and wishful thinking. Those guys want to come home as much as we want them back, so the rumors are flying." *And who's Jill's husband?*

Then there's silence. Not the friendly lull in the conversation, but tense, unhappy silence. *I can almost hear the countdown in my head— 3, 2, 1.* "So when *will* they be back?" *And we have lift-off.*

"I don't know, Jane. I'm sorry. As soon as I hear anything official I'm going to call all of you and let you know. I promise."

More silence. "OK. Thanks. I just want him home."

"I know. Me too."

It would be another two months before they came home.

# Chapter 10

# HOMECOMING

Paul and I celebrated our third wedding anniversary on May 6, 2003, half a world apart. He called twice: once when it was the sixth in Iraq and once when it was the sixth in California. He also managed, with the help of a satellite phone call to my dad, to send me roses. Peach roses—the same type that I carried on our wedding day. I think he scored more points with me for actually remembering the type of flowers in my bouquet than he did for sending the flowers. But it was a bittersweet day—wonderful because Paul remembered our anniversary and was able to call, sad because I sat alone that night watching our wedding video.

By now it looked like the unit would be on its way home soon. Days were being suggested and discarded. We were hoping to have them home by the end of the month. Emily's first birthday was coming up on June 27, and I really wanted Paul home for it. She had been standing on her own and cruising around furniture for months. Every time she tried to take a step on her own I would swoop in and pick her up. She was so close to walking, but I didn't want Paul to miss her first steps. After everything else he had missed, I wanted him to see that. As the days kept passing and there was no definite date for the reunion, I was starting to feel guilty for deliberately stunting my daughter's growth. I decided I was going to wait until June to see if Paul would make it home and then let her go for it.

It was the second week in May (or so) when we got the good news. They had planes scheduled for the end of the month. Yeah! My husband was coming home. But there was a catch. They were getting out of Iraq before the other

Twentynine Palms units because in December they were going to deploy to Okinawa for seven months. I think most of us turned into Scarlett O'Hara when we heard that—"I'll think of it all tomorrow." Let's just get them home first and deal with the rest later.

Once again, phones were ringing off the hook. Only one phone call really sticks out in my mind from that crazy time. It was from the wife of one of Paul's Marines.

"Michelle? It's Sharon." (Again, not her real name, but an actual conversation.) "Is it true they're coming home in a few weeks?"

"Yes, isn't it great?"

"No. No, he can't come home already."

*Uhh . . . careful.* "Why not? Don't you want to see Bill again?"

"Of course, but he's going to be so pissed at me."

*Uh-oh.* "Why?" *Oh God, what was it? Cheating? Weight gain? Dramatic hair-dye job?*

"I haven't saved any money. I spent all of his combat pay!"

Now this was not uncommon. I think the Marines were taking bets on whose wife had spent the most or saved the most during the deployment. Just part of the war-time fun.

Aside from money worries, everyone calling wanted specific days and times for when the guys would be back. When would the buses get to the base, when could we pick up our Marine and split? And here we were met with the wall of military uncertainty; everything about the return flights was up in the air. They were scheduled to leave on this day and arrive on that day, but so much can happen between now and then. And we had no idea who was going to be on which flight.

It became an exercise in frustration for everyone. I had family members calling from all over the country who wanted to be there to meet the buses when their husband/son/brother/cousin/boyfriend got back. When should they book their flights? Where could they stay? When would the Marines go on leave? Could I guarantee they'd be back on this day or during this week? It was chaos. And all we could tell people was to call the hotline.

The battalion had a toll-free number set up with a recorded message giving as much information as the rear party had. I told people over and over to keep checking the hotline for updates. Once we, the Key Volunteers, received copies of the flight manifests (that were subject to change until the planes left the ground), we called all the wives and told them which flight their husband was scheduled to be on. After that, we told them to call the hotline for specific times and to not get too focused on one day or time; everything will change at least once.

We also planned a reunion brief for the wives. A reunion brief is an event that all units are required to stage for family members before the Marines return from a deployment— not just combat deployments, any deployment. It is meant to give the wives an idea of what to expect when they are reunited with their husbands. Marine Corps Community Services (MCCS) did most of the work for us and put together a host of speakers. Staff Sergeant Garcia was there to speak for the command and answer questions that were specific to the Three-Four Marines (you know—when will they get here?).

One of the first things the speakers bluntly told us was not to expect a second honeymoon. We had been separated from our husbands for months, and when they came home there was going to be a period of adjustment. And it might not be pretty. We had to be prepared to get to know each other again, to get used to living with each other again. I will admit, I felt pretty smug listening to that. After all, Paul and I had already been apart for six months during TBS. We'd be fine. Right?

Then when the MCCS speaker started talking about children, I perked up a bit. How would Emily adjust to having her daddy back? How would I adjust? I had a routine, I had a daily plan. Good Lord, I was going to have to cook again.

Then one of the base chaplains stood up to give us the sex talk. (Poor guy, having to stand in front of a room—coincidentally a chapel—full of wives, most of whom had kids but who were not above a healthy dose of the giggles, and talk about sex.) Most of the women I knew (and, yes, I was one of them) had already done a good bit of shopping in the Victoria's Secret catalog. But the chaplain said we shouldn't get our hopes up for that second-honeymoon sex. We should allow for time to reestablish intimacy before expecting our sex lives to pick up where they left off. His advice to us was to take it slow. We shouldn't expect too much of our Marines or ourselves. (I had a six-month-old when my husband left, so there wasn't much of a sex life to pick up.)

As for me, I was excited and nervous at the same time. I didn't know what to expect. I was hoping that Paul and I would be able to jump right back into our married life and that everything would be just like it was before. (With maybe a bit more romance since Emily was finally sleeping through the night.) Maybe the war would simply fade away like a bad dream. But part of me knew that wouldn't happen. After the chaplain's warning, we got another one. This one was from Larry Stratton, an MCCS civilian who was also a former Marine. His warning was a bit more explicit.

"Ladies, a word about meeting your Marines at the reunion site. Think carefully about what you want to wear. Save the miniskirts and bikini tops for when you get home." (So much for showing up in my leopard-print teddy.) "And try to save the reunion sex for when you get home too." He then went on to tell a story from his Marine days about when he returned home from a deployment. Apparently one anxious wife had rented a limo to meet her husband, and that limo was bouncing before the other Marines had finished collecting their sea bags. That had not gone over well with the Marine's command—a little inappropriate.

Considering the fact that I'd be bringing my baby with me, I thought I could manage to meet Paul without looking like a bimbo or being tempted to have sex in the car.

Staff Sergeant Garcia gave us as much information as he had on the flights. Paul was on the last flight (of course), and it was scheduled to come in on May 23. That was only two weeks away.

Those two weeks flew by. I barely had time to sit and think about Paul actually being home again. I was so anxious and excited, I couldn't sit still. With all my nervous energy, I cleaned and re-cleaned my already clean house. I wanted everything to be perfect for Paul when he came home. Would he like the new curtains in the family room? Would he like my longer hair? What would he think of Emily? What would he think of me? Would he still love me the same way? It had been over four months since we had seen each other. How much had changed? I was so excited to have him finally coming home, but there was also an anxious flutter in my stomach at the thought of our reunion. It felt a lot like our wedding day—I was happy, excited, and nervous all at the same time. And it wasn't just me. Those days leading up to the reunion were chaotic for everyone. People were passing vacuums and floor buffers back and forth. Half the women I knew were going on a crash diet, and nearly everyone was getting a haircut and a manicure. My shopping list, which had been minimal for months, suddenly doubled. I stocked up on steaks, beer, and coffee. I planned out all of Paul's favorite dinners and baked up a storm. When he called a week before he was due to leave Iraq, I asked what he wanted to eat when he got back. He wanted fresh fruit and beer—together probably would have been OK with him. He sounded so tired and ready to come home.

On May 20, just a few days before Paul was scheduled to return, I ignored my thirtieth birthday. I had decided that I was going to put off turning thirty until my husband came home. Paul called and said we'd celebrate when he got home in a few days. That was the best present, knowing I'd have my husband home again in just a matter of days. Having your husband go to war is a pretty good way to avoid looking thirty straight in the eye. None of my friends wanted to harass me about it, and I was too emotionally drained to worry about it. So I slipped gently out of my twenties and thought more about the next week than the next decade.

It's a tradition when a unit returns from a deployment for military families to cover the base with welcome-home signs—big signs, little signs, plain signs, and complicated signs. In Twentynine Palms, there is a really long chain-link fence that runs along the main road leading to the front gate and out into town. A few days before Three-Four was due to come home, the signs started appearing there. It was one of the coolest things I have ever seen in my life. The main road on base was covered with words of love.

"Welcome Home, SSgt. Jones. I love you."

"Cpl. Richards. I love you."

"I missed you, Daddy. Capt. Smith."

"Lt. Hill, your son can't wait to meet you."

"Three-Four Rocks!"

"Motor T Marines job well done."

"Sgt. London, I'm so proud of you."

Everywhere you looked on base, there was a sign. And it wasn't just on base. Out in town, the community had come together to support our Marines. Signs were in store windows; yellow ribbons were tied on trees and telephone poles. There was a huge billboard that read, "Twentynine Palms supports our Marines and Sailors."

I made four signs for Paul. The first two I hung on the chain-link fence along the road on base. One sign was from Emily and said, "Lt. Keener. I love you, Daddy!" The other was from me and said, "Lt. Keener. SHMILY." That's our thing—SHMILY. It stands for "See How Much I Love You." I knew Paul would understand. I hung the other two signs on our garage door. One was a copy of the famous picture of Paul and the Iraqi girl, and it said "My Daddy, My Hero. Love Emily." The other was from me and said "Paul, I'm so proud to be your wife."

But there also was controversy over the signs. One wife in our battalion hung a sign for her husband that ended up having to come down. She was in H&S Company, so Staff Sergeant Garcia called me to ask me to give her the news.

"Michelle, have you seen the sign Mrs. Smith (not her real name) made for her husband?"

"There are a lot of signs out there, Fabian. I don't know, maybe."

"Oh, you'd remember this one. Can you call her and tell her she needs to take it down?"

"Take it down? Why? What's wrong with it?" *I can hear him starting to chuckle.*

"PMO [military police] has received some complaints about it."

"Why? What does it say?"

Staff Sergeant Garcia gave an embarrassed chuckle. "It says, 'Cpl. Smith . . . come get some lovin'.'"

I stop and think about that for a minute. "That doesn't seem so bad."

More chuckling. "She misspelled 'come.'"

Pause. Think. Understand. "Ohhh." Then I start to laugh. "I'm not calling her."

"Please don't make me do it."

I love it when big tough Marines are terrified of military wives.

"Come on, Michelle."

Then we both start laughing again. In the end I refused to bail him out, and he had to make the call. Mrs. Smith took down her sign and replaced it with something less . . . imaginative.

Paul's flight ended up being delayed until the twenty-fourth. And even then the arrival time back on base went from 11 a.m. to 1 p.m. to 5 p.m. I just kept calling the hotline and waiting for news that the buses had left the airfield. Once again, it ended up being the wives' grapevine that gave me the heads up. About 3 p.m., Jennifer called me. Her husband had come home a few weeks earlier as part of the advance party (and he was right by her side the following month when their baby girl was born), so he was in the loop on the buses coming back to base.

"Michelle, it's Jennifer. Have you heard?"

"Heard what?"

"They're here."

"What, now?"

"They made good time. They're at the armory right now dropping off their weapons before they head up to the gym."

"OK. I'm on my way. Thanks."

Oh my God, oh my God, oh my God! He was here.

Back on base. I need to go. Gotta get up there before the buses arrive. Where's Emily? Where's the diaper bag? What am I going to wear?

The reunion was taking place in the parking lot outside of the east gym on base. I had been there only once before, and in the back of my mind was a fear that I wouldn't be able to find it again. I had this ridiculous fantasy of Paul stepping off the bus, happy to be home, and I'd still be driving around base trying to find the stupid gym. Fortunately I had a map of the base taped to my refrigerator (big help when wives called me to ask for directions to somewhere). If Jennifer called at three o'clock, I was out the door with Emily by 3:15. We drove up to the gym, parked, and joined the crowds.

It was packed. I had opted to put Emily in the stroller, and once we made it into the crush of people, I was very glad I had. The Marine band was there playing. Hundreds of people had crushed into the parking lot, some with banners, signs, personalized T-shirts. It was like a carnival. This was the last group of Marines from Three-Four to return home; there were about 200 Marines coming in and probably 400 people waiting for them.

Outside I found Jessica, Lynde, Krista, and Jennifer. Because Tony had already come home, Jennifer had designated herself official photographer for the reunions. The rest of us were nervously waiting for our husbands. Jessica and Lynde had dressed up in gorgeous black sundresses. For a moment I wished I had thought of it, but then I looked at Emily in her stroller and the diaper bag over my shoulder and realized my dressing-up days might be gone. I felt better when I saw Krista, also in casual clothes. She was holding her baby boy who had been born only six weeks before the battalion deployed. She said, "I have a baby and I'm here. That's enough." I love Krista.

As I walked around, pushing Emily, I was stopped by a reporter. He was holding his microphone and had a cameraman behind him.

"Excuse me, is your husband coming home today?"

"Yes, he is."

"How old is your baby?"

"She's eleven months."

"Oh," he says with disappointment. "So she was pretty big when he left."

"Well, she was six months."

"OK. Never mind." And he walked away. When I met up with Jennifer and the KVs, I told them what happened.

"He's just looking for a sob story," Lynde said practically.

I also bumped into Major Baker. He had also come home earlier with the advance party. He gave me a big hug and thanked me for all the work I had done with the KVs. He and Paul had ridden in the same vehicle during the entire deployment, so he shared some stories with me and had me laughing in no time. It was good to see him back home with Ann.

We ended up waiting nearly two hours. When Emily had had enough of sitting in the stroller, I ended up holding her. She was just starting to get heavy when we heard the news that the buses were on the way.

Suddenly there was new life in the fading crowd. Our little group started pushing closer to the edge of the parking lot, and we were all straining to catch the first glimpse of the buses. We saw them start to crawl up the hill, and everyone cheered. I was already tearing up, and I was glad I wasn't the only one. The Marine band started playing something patriotic that I can't remember now, and we all waved. I can't remember ever being in the midst of such excitement—it was infectious. Parents were waving signs, children were being lifted up to see over the crowd, wives were already calling out their husbands' names.

When the buses turned, went past the gym, and disappeared around the corner, I thought we might be looking at a riot. Fortunately, Major Baker was still standing with us, and he explained that they were going to circle the gym and come back down so that the doors opened facing the crowd and the Marines didn't have to walk around the bus. That may have been the logical plan, but logic doesn't mean much to a group of anxious wives. It was another fifteen minutes more before the buses finally reached us.

The band broke into the Marines' hymn, and the doors opened. The crowd screamed when the first Marines stepped off the buses. My vision was fuzzy from tears as I watched Marines step down and find their loved ones. Wives were breaking away from the crowd and running to meet their husbands. Marines were dropping their bags and scooping up children they hadn't seen in months, to the cries of "Daddy! Daddy you're home." Mother and fathers held their sons that they had worried over, cried for.

We were all searching every face that came down. There were three buses, and I didn't want to miss Paul. How would he find Emily and me? I held her tightly as the crowd pushed past me. I kept scanning the bus doors.

"There's Russell!" Lynde yelled spotting Krista's husband. "Where's Krista?"

We all started yelling. "Krista! Krista! Russell's here—he's over there." I watched as she turned, saw her husband, and smiled. She was crying when he wrapped his arms around her and his son who had grown so much in four months.

"There's Nick!" We found Jessica's husband and started waving him over. Jessica squealed when he made his way over. Then out of nowhere, Jay appeared behind Lynde and gave her a huge hug. And suddenly, I was alone, watching and waiting.

Then I saw him. He was one of the last to get off the bus. I screamed his name and waved. I knew the moment he saw me. He pushed his way through the crowd. Just a few feet from me, a man handing out beers to the Marines stopped him. I remember thinking, *You stopped for a beer?* Then he was right there in front of me, and I forgot everything else.

I don't know who was around us, I don't know what the band was playing. All I remember is that he put his arms around me and held on tight.

"Welcome home, Marine."

Later I would be forever thankful for Jennifer who captured the moment on film and gave me a copy of the picture.

"God, I missed you," he said quietly. Then he pulled back and looked at Emily. "She's so big." He tried to take her and hold her, but she started crying and reached for me. His face, already lined with fatigue, dropped. "She doesn't remember me, does she?"

How do you tell a man that his daughter—the little girl he thought of every day for months—that he ached with missing, didn't know who he was?

"She will," I said. "Just give her time, it's been a crazy day."

"Yeah, let's just go."

I had thought we would need to check in with somebody, or that Paul would want to track down some of his Marines, but he just wanted to go home. As I looked around I noticed that there wasn't much socializing going on at all. People found their loved ones and took off as quickly as possible. The Marines that didn't have anyone meeting the buses were slowly walking back to their barracks.

"Didn't you want to say good-bye to anyone?" I asked as we started toward the car.

"Honey, I've seen these guys every day for the past four months. Right now, I just want to see you and Emily."

We did see people on the way to the car. A few of his Marines stopped us to introduce their wives to Paul. I was so proud of the way Paul always had something nice to say to each wife about the work her husband had done.

When we got to the car and put Emily in her car seat, Paul opened the passenger door for me.

"Do you want me to drive?" I asked.

"Why?"

"Well, you just got home."

Then he smiled. The first real smile I'd seen in months. "I haven't forgotten how to drive."

We got home, and I called my mom and dad to let them know Paul was back safe. The general consensus was that they'd leave us alone for a day to just be together. Then the calls and questions and stories would start.

I put Emily to bed and told her that her daddy was home. Afterward, Paul and I talked for a while, but not about the war. He didn't notice the new curtains or the fact that I had shampooed the carpet. He didn't notice my hair was longer than when he had left or that I had lost five pounds. And I didn't care. He was home. That was what mattered. It was as if he stepped into the house, took a deep breath, and just relaxed—for probably the first time in four months. We sat on the sofa and held each other, and I could see that he was exhausted. I finally told him to go to bed, but he didn't want to leave me.

"I'll be here in the morning," I said.

Paul took a really long, hot shower and then fell asleep. Sometime during the night he rolled into me. He startled awake.

"Who's there?"

"It's me, Michelle. Your wife?"

"Oh. OK." Then he went back to sleep.

The next morning, Emily crawled over to him. She held his hand, stood up, and took her first steps. I have a picture of that, too.

# Chapter 11

# COOKING FOR TWO

My house was messy again. I love my husband, and I was so happy to have him back, but my house was messy again. I'm a neat freak, bordering on compulsive and during the deployment my house had been nearly spotless. I knew where everything was, all the toys were put away every night, my kitchen was always clean. In one day, that was gone.

The morning after Paul came home he turned his sea bag upside down and shook everything out onto the floor; it looked like I had some laundry to do. His uniforms, right down to the underwear, were sent to the garage. I wanted to burn everything, but he had developed an attachment to the uniforms he had worn during the war.

"But they're filthy," I protested.

"Yeah," he agreed with a grin. "But they make me look salty."

So the uniforms were spared. I washed them five or six times and pronounced them fit for the closet. But socks and shorts were thrown away (remember, he had gone for weeks at a time without a shower). Uniforms I could handle, but the underwear—no way.

I had actually put together a welcome-home gift basket that Paul opened the day after he returned. In it was an assortment of new socks and underwear (I had been planning this purging). My mom had also put together a gift basket full of gag gifts like soap, razors, deodorant, and a huge bottle of Baileys Irish Cream.

I had also redecorated the office in our house for him as a surprise. I had framed and hung up all of his military awards (and there were many—he's been in the service since the age of seventeen). Right in the middle of what I like to call his "glory wall" was an eight-by-ten copy of the picture of him and the Iraqi girl. I had ordered two copies of it from the Associated Press, one for us and one for his mother. Paul looked at that picture for a long time. "I wonder what happened to her."

It didn't take much for us to adjust to being back together, but there were a few awkward moments. He didn't know anything about Emily's routine or the rules I had set for her. If she started jabbering about a special toy, he didn't know what she wanted. And though she quickly warmed back up to him, she still wanted me most of the time. For the most part, Paul just watched in amazement at everything she had learned to do while he had been gone. She was running along the edges of furniture, she was standing on her own, she was using words we could actually understand. I know he's proud of the work he did in Iraq, but I think there's a part of him that will always regret missing as much as he did. But then he'll say, "That's part of the job," and he'll move on. I admire the hell out of that man.

It took a few days for Paul and me to get back to that "married for a few years" comfort level we had before, but we got there. For a few weeks, we spent most of our time just talking about what we each had done over the past few months. Paul shared funny stories, good times, but he didn't want to talk about the ugliness. I knew he had seen death, I knew he had experienced fear, but he wasn't ready to talk about it. I didn't know if he'd ever want to talk about it.

I told him about what life had been like back in Twentynine Palms. I showed him all the pictures I had taken of Emily. I got to spin stories about the things that had happened on base, the funny and sad phone calls I had received from wives and family members. It was almost like a first date, where you sit across from each other and share your life stories—except we were already married, so we knew who we were going home with. And while we may not have had second-honeymoon sex, we did just fine.

Paul had to go back to work for a few days the week he returned, and then he was able to take leave. We didn't go anywhere. Most of our friends who came back from Iraq took leave and went home to visit family or took long vacations to Ireland, Hawaii, or the Caribbean. We stayed on base. And it was perfect. We took Emily to the park, and Paul played his way back into her heart. I relearned how to cook. During the deployment I had lived on sandwiches, cereal, and ice cream. Now I was once again using more than just the microwave. We also had family come to visit us. I think they all wanted to see for themselves that Paul was alive and in one piece. We had a small family celebration for Emily's first birthday, and Paul went nuts on gifts for her. Our family was whole again.

But we knew it was only for a short time. The battalion was scheduled to leave for a seven-month deployment to Okinawa in December. They were leaving before Christmas. We tried not to think of it for the first few months Paul was home, but it was always there: a date on the calendar looming in the distance.

There was a definite split among the wives in dealing with the upcoming deployment. Most of us tried to be positive about it: "Hey, it could be worse. They could be going back to Iraq." But a vocal minority was outraged that the guys were only going to be home for six months and then be sent off again. Of course it sucked—I knew that, but there wasn't anything we could do about it.

By July, 2003, the battalion was back to the same hard and fast training schedule they had had the year before. In August they were gone for a month of training, and that was a very difficult time for families. Our men were home from war, but even when they were home, they weren't. They were training long days, they were in the field, they were gone for long stretches at a time. There was a lot of tension among the wives—which of course led to tension for the Marines. It was like the old adage says, "If she's not happy, no one's happy."

In the midst of this chaos, there was also a lot of turnover in the battalion—Marines leaving, new Marines coming in—and this meant turnover for the Key Volunteer Network as well. Lynde and Jessica were moving; Stephanie and Erika decided they'd had enough and left the group. Major Baker, the executive officer, was leaving the battalion, so Ann would be stepping down as the KV advisor. There was a great deal of speculation about the new XO. If he were married, his wife would probably take over as the KV advisor. Of course she wasn't officially obligated, but we figured that was how it would work out. But it ended up that the new guy was a bachelor. Krista took over as the KV advisor, which left the KV coordinator position vacant.

"Sure," I said. "I'll do it."

In all fairness, I volunteered myself this time. Again, all I can say is that it seemed like a good idea at the time.

In September, 2003, we had our first meeting with the new group. There was Krista and me, Jennifer, Monica Langella (who was now expecting her first baby), Monica Coughlin, and Mary Pittman back for another deployment. We also added Kristy Hayes, the wife of a sergeant in Kilo Company and mother of three little girls; Jo Rosbough (without a doubt the most elegant woman I have ever met and wife of the Weapons Company first sergeant), who was the secretary for the base commanding general and able to get her hands on all kinds of information for us when we needed it; Venus Martinez-Robinson, married to a staff sergeant in Kilo Company and a take-no-prisoners-lets-get-it-done kind of woman; Rebecca Hammond, the young wife of one of Paul's Marines, who came on board to take over the communications platoon for me; and Alli Jimenez, the wife of one of the battalion's supply officers. Alli was quiet and shy, the mother of three. She didn't participate much in the meetings, but she wanted to help out.

The biggest change in the group was the executive officer. Major Baker attended our first meeting and introduced his successor. The XO was also the family readiness officer (FRO), and as the KV coordinator I would be working closely with him; though the Key Volunteers work directly for the battalion commanding officer, our main point of contact is the FRO. So if we got an XO who wasn't very sympathetic to the KVN or didn't give much of a thought to the families of the unit, we could be in serious trouble.

My first thought as Major Baker introduced Major Andy Petrucci was, "This can't be good."

Major Petrucci didn't say much during the meeting, but he was watching us closely. From his very short, high and tight haircut to his you–don't–impress–me expression, he was Marine through and through. If Matt Baker could have posed for *GQ*, Andy Petrucci would have told the photographer how to run the shoot more efficiently. He wasn't married, and I wondered how understanding a bachelor could be to the needs of the battalion families.

After the meeting, Krista and I huddled together to compare notes. We both decided that since Lieutenant Colonel McCoy really seemed to like Major Petrucci, we'd give him the benefit of the doubt.

We decided to put together another social event for the wives of the unit. We wanted to get as many wives as we could to attend to meet Lieutenant Colonel McCoy and the KVs, so we planned out appropriate bribery to get them there, including a day off for their husbands, free food, and door prizes. We knew with the Okinawa deployment looming in the distance, there may be questions or concerns that we could address. The event,

Spouse Appreciation Night, was planned for October.

Krista and I decided to meet at her house a few weeks before the event to figure out what we wanted to say. While I was there, Krista also confided some big news.

"Michelle," she began. "I should tell you this since in a few months it will affect you a lot. I'm pregnant."

My first honest thought was, *You're a better woman than me.* Emily was still an only child, and after having been a single mom during a deployment I figured she'd probably stay that way. Fortunately, I managed not to stick my foot in my mouth and said instead, "Congratulations! That's wonderful!" I gave her a big hug. "When are you due?"

"In April."

"That's so exciting. Did you guys plan it?"

Krista rolled her eyes and shook her head. "No. We planned on having more kids, just not this close together." Her son, Kyle, was only ten months old at the time. "Remember when the guys were in Bridgeport in August? Russell was only home for one night."

"Well," I said thoughtfully, "I guess we all know what you two were doing."

Krista laughed. "Yeah. So, in April I may be out of commission for a while. That means you'll have to take over pretty much everything in the KVN. Are you going to be OK with that? Because we can try to find you a co-coordinator if you want."

"No, Krista, don't worry, I'll be fine. They're just going to be hanging out in Okinawa. It won't be like last time."

"Thank God for that."

The Spouse Appreciation Night was held in one of the large rooms in the Protestant chapel on base. As the wives arrived, there was a definite difference in their faces from the event we had held the year before. The Marines had only been home for four months, and they were leaving again in less than three months. Many of the wives were far less friendly to anyone in uniform than they had been before. Krista and I handled the introductions of the KVs and then let Lieutenant Colonel McCoy take the floor. After his brief speech, he took questions.

"Is Three-Four going back to Iraq?"

"Ladies," the CO began. "As of right now we are scheduled to go to Okinawa for seven months. Anything you hear about Iraq is strictly rumor." *(Where have I heard that before?)*

A number of young wives had been staring daggers at Lieutenant Colonel McCoy. The man was no longer just their husband's boss, he was the guy taking their husband away from home. One of them demanded, "Are there any more field exercises coming up? My husband is gone all the time."

"We have a few more training exercises scheduled, but we also have block leave available in November. So your husbands will be able to take some time off before we deploy."

"Do you have to go before Christmas?" asked another wife, and the bitterness level of the room instantly went up.

"My husband is advance party. He'll be gone before Thanksgiving."

"Can't you push it back two weeks?"

"Will my husband be able to come home when my baby is born?"

Poor Lieutenant Colonel McCoy. I don't think there's anything more frightening to a man than a room full of angry women. The man could yank down the statue of a dictator in Baghdad, but these wives were going for blood. He did his best to answer their questions, but there was a definite chill in the air. Eventually we let him off the hook and moved on to awarding the door prizes. As the prizes were being announced, I went over to talk to the CO.

"I don't think I'm their favorite person anymore," he said.

"Doesn't look like it, sir," I agreed. "I can walk you out to your car if you want. Just in case any of them tries to jump you."

He smiled and laughed. "I may take you up on that. Thanks."

"No problem, sir."

"Michelle." He looked at me seriously. "You know you can call me Bryan." *Uh-huh . . . I don't see that happening . . . sir.* "OK. Thanks." (I don't think I called him anything from that point on.)

"So," I said, changing the subject, "I hear General Mattis really likes Three-Four." Paul had told me that Jim Mattis, commanding general of 1st Marine Division, had been trying some fancy footwork to get Three-Four to go back over to Iraq instead of Okinawa.

"He likes our style," Lieutenant Colonel McCoy replied proudly.

"Is that the 'destroy everything in our path' style?" I teased.

"That's the one."

General Mattis had visited Twentynine Palms during the Iraq deployment. He was a quiet, older man, but as tough as they come. And he wasn't married.

"You know, I think I should fix General Mattis up with my mother," I said casually to the CO.

I don't think I've ever seen a man turn so pale so fast. "Please don't," was all he said.

Of course, the Spouse Appreciation Night wasn't the last time Lieutenant Colonel McCoy had to face the wives of Three-Four. In November, 2003, just before the block leave period began, we held a pre-deployment brief to prepare the families as much as possible for the deployment. We explained about communication with Okinawa and the training schedule the guys would have over there. A number of wives asked about the possibility of accompanying their husbands to Okinawa, but we explained that it just wasn't feasible. We also reminded them to be sure they knew where all the important financial information was located, and we encouraged the Marines to give their wives power of attorney for things like taxes and bills. We also mentioned that the wives should get a special power of attorney with regard to their children. During the last deployment a wife in another unit had been killed in a car accident while her husband was in Iraq. There was no plan in place for someone to take custody of their children, so they had been placed in foster care. To avoid this, we suggested that the wives designate someone local to take immediate custody of the children and then maybe a family member, who may live further away, to come in and take custody until their husband could come home. I asked my friend Justine to take Emily in case anything happened to me, and I made sure she knew how to reach my mom and dad. We also talked about all the services on base available to families and reintroduced the KVs for each company.

After the informational part of the evening, Lieutenant Colonel McCoy once again had to face the wives. And once again, Iraq was the first question he faced.

"Are you *sure* you're not going back to Iraq?"

"Ladies, we are going to Okinawa. There was talk of us going back to Iraq, but the decision had been made to send us to Okinawa." What he didn't mention was that most of the Marines would probably have preferred going to Iraq. I know Paul was disappointed that they weren't going to get back in the fight, and I'd bet my last dollar that the CO felt the same. Marines are such, well, *Marines*.

The wives were in a better mood after that meeting. Block leave was coming up, so we'd all have some time with our husbands before they left. And Okinawa didn't seem too bad. As Jennifer said when she and I discussed the deployment, "After going through the stress of Iraq, dealing with Okinawa will be a piece of cake."

And really we were all anticipating a much less stressful few months. Many of us were planning trips to

Okinawa to visit while the guys were over there. Paul joked that he was going to spend his free-time scuba diving and hiking. And though it was disappointing that the length of the Okinawa deployment had been extended from six months to seven, I kept telling myself if wouldn't be that bad. After all, nothing could be as terrible as going through a combat deployment. At least in Okinawa no one would be shooting at him.

# Chapter 12

# HERE WE GO AGAIN

He did it again. Paul came home in the middle of the workday. I should have known then what he was going to say, but I didn't.

"I need to tell you something," he said.

"OK. What's going on?"

"We're going back to Iraq."

*He did not just say Iraq.* "What about Okinawa?"

"We're going there first for about six weeks then we're heading over to Iraq for the rest of the deployment."

*This cannot be happening. Not again.* "Are you serious? Lieutenant Colonel McCoy was so sure you guys were going to miss it." *I don't know if I can do this again—the worry, the waiting. He made it home once, but what if he doesn't come back this time?*

"General Mattis requested us personally." I could hear the pride in his voice. And beneath the pride there was excitement. He was excited to be getting back in the fight. Maybe he didn't want to leave his family again, but I knew, deep down, he would have picked Iraq over Okinawa any day. And in that moment I wanted to scream at him for not being upset or sad or angry that he was going back into combat.

"Looks like I picked the wrong time to take over as KV coordinator," I said.

Just a few days after Paul told me the news, I took two new KVs in to meet Lieutenant Colonel McCoy and Major Petrucci. Lieutenant Colonel McCoy brought us into his office. The two KVs sat together on the large sofa facing his desk, and I sat on a smaller sofa. By now I had become more comfortable with him and made myself at home, but I noticed my two new KVs sat right next to each other and barely said a word. Had I been that nervous around him at first? Who am I kidding? I had been terrified.

The CO sat himself down on the coffee table in front of us. He was very warm and welcoming, and he did his best to put the new KVs at ease. Then he started talking about the upcoming deployment. Though the point of the meeting was to introduce the new KVs, this was also the first chance I'd had to talk to Lieutenant Colonel McCoy about the new deployment plan.

"I know this change may make things difficult for all of you volunteers," the CO said. "I wish we had known about it earlier. I don't want the wives to think I was lying to them at the pre-deployment brief. We just found out a few days ago."

The new KVs nodded silently.

"Don't worry, sir," I said. "We'll be fine. Is there anything specific you want us to work on with the families?"

"Just show your courage," he said. "The Marines need to know that their families are being taken care of so they can focus on their jobs. If the families back home fall apart, the Marines won't be able to keep it together. We really need all of you to show your courage to the American people. We need you to be strong so that the enemy will have no reason to think they're winning."

"Show your courage" became the unofficial theme for the KVN during this deployment. In our monthly newsletter, I included a section on dealing with the media so that everyone would be prepared. By this time the national media was leaning away from the patriotic show of support for the war and toward criticizing President Bush and our presence in Iraq. A few months into the deployment the Commandant of the Marine Corps and the Sergeant Major of the Marine Corps came to Twentynine Palms to visit with the families of deployed Marines. One of the things the Sergeant Major said was how impressed he was that he never saw a Marine wife on television complaining about the deployments. We could take pride in the fact that our husbands were tough, and many times we were tougher.

By the time the block-leave period rolled around, the KVN had already started getting in touch with wives. We wanted to make sure we weren't going to miss anyone when we needed to make phone calls.

By then Major Andy Petrucci and I had been working together for a few months. We were now on a first-name basis and had slipped into a good rhythm. It involved a lot of sarcasm, and fortunately he and I shared a slightly warped sense of humor. In spite of my initial concerns, he turned out to be a blessing. He took the work of the KVN seriously.

Less than a month before the battalion was due to leave, the new regimental CO, Colonel Craig Tucker, held a brief for all the KVs of the units who would be deploying. His wife, Elizabeth, had taken over as the new regimental KV advisor, and we would be able to meet her as well. Krista didn't make it, but a few of our other KVs did. I ended up sitting next to Jennifer and right in front of Lieutenant Colonel McCoy and Andy. The four of us listened politely to Colonel Tucker's speech and to the information guys, but we really acted like the bad kids in the room. Our guys already had their departure date— they were the first ones leaving. We already had our orders, so we were in the back in the room whispering and feeling pretty smug. When it came time for questions, Jennifer had one of the first ones.

"Will there be reporters embedded with the units again? Specifically Three-Four?"

"Good question," Colonel Tucker replied. "We will have reporters with some of the units again. I don't have the assignments yet, but we'll be following up with that so we can prevent some of the shit that happened the last time." Oops! He said the "s" word. Lieutenant Colonel McCoy cracked up, and Colonel Tucker cast a sheepish glance at his wife.

Andy leaned forward and whispered to Jennifer and me, "Elizabeth is going to yell at him for that one."

I looked at Jennifer, "Look what you did. You made him swear!"

As the questions went on, I leaned back and asked Lieutenant Colonel McCoy if the battalion would be coming straight home from Iraq or if it was going to have to go back to Okinawa before coming home to Twentynine Palms. He said they'd be coming straight home.

But was that good enough for me? Guess not, because I raised my hand a few minutes later.

"Colonel Tucker, Three-Four is going to Okinawa before they head to Iraq. Will they be able to come straight home when they finish their deployment, or will they have to go back to Okinawa first?"

Lieutenant Colonel McCoy leaned forward. "Don't you trust me?" he teased.

"I trust you—I don't trust the people who outrank you."

But Colonel Tucker gave the same answer: the unit would not have to detour to Okinawa on its way back home. At least that was one bit of good news.

During the preparation for the deployment, I was becoming a fixture at the battalion headquarters. One time I stopped by to drop off something for Russell Boyce to take home to Krista. When I got to the building I wasn't sure where to find the Weapons Company section. I stopped a young Marine and asked where to find Major Boyce. As he was pointing me in the right direction, the battalion sergeant major came up to us.

"Is there a problem?" Sergeant Major Dave Howell demanded. (This sergeant major doesn't ask anything, he demands.)

"No, sergeant major," the Marine stammered. "Mrs. Keener was just looking for Major Boyce." (Russell had been promoted just a few weeks earlier.) "I've got it," the sergeant major said and started to lead me out the door and across to the Weapons Company building. "And next time," he added gruffly to the Marine, "you escort her over there."

I didn't know Sergeant Major Howell very well. He was a rough, tough, solid piece of man. Paul respected the hell out of him, and nearly everyone lived in fear of him. As we walked I mentioned to him that I had seen him in the *National Geographic* documentary on Three-Four's role during Operation Iraqi Freedom (OIF).

"My dad was really impressed with you," I said.

"Oh, that was all bullshit," he replied gruffly. And that was the end of it. When we reached the Weapons Company building, he opened the door for me, stepped in, and boomed, "Everybody proper. There's a lady on deck." I decided I really liked the man.

When I found Russell's office, he wasn't there, so I just left the information for Krista on his desk. As I was leaving, Sergeant Major Howell introduced me to Gunnery Sergeant (or "Gunny") Robert Justice, who was going to be in charge of the rear party during the deployment. He wanted to go over the KV roster with me and make sure he had everyone's information. Gunny Justice had a moustache; now, you don't often see Marines with moustaches, so it took me by surprise. He also seemed ready to take over once the battalion left and willing to support the Key Volunteer Network. That was comforting.

The final month leading up to the deployment flew by. I had more meetings with Krista, Lieutenant Colonel McCoy, and Andy. One night we had our meeting out at the Twentynine Palms Inn, which was pretty much the only actual restaurant in town. (Krista and I joked that we left our husbands home to babysit so we could go on a double date with their bosses. That joke didn't go over well with the men left behind to change diapers, but

Krista and I enjoyed it.) It was at this meeting that I learned that Lieutenant Colonel McCoy had met his wife, Kerry, at the starting line of the Marine Corps marathon. They ran and talked for about sixteen miles, then he waited for her at the finish line. Truly romantic, in a masochistic, running-26.2-miles kind of way. And I suppose once you've seen each other at the end of a marathon it all gets better from there.

I finally got to meet Kerry McCoy in November at the annual Marine Corps Birthday Ball, which celebrates the founding of the Marine Corps. The first one I attended was just five months after our wedding, and it reminded me a lot of prom. Everyone gets all dressed up, there are formal pictures, and there is dinner and dancing. The Three-Four ball this year was held in Las Vegas. OK, not actually in Las Vegas. We were actually in the first hotel on the Nevada side of the state line. But there was still plenty of alcohol and gambling. My mom had come out to watch Emily so we could go. It was my first night away from my daugher, and I only called home to check on her ten or twenty times.

During the ball they showed a slide presentation of Three-Four's exploits during OIF. There were cheers and shouts when they showed pictures of the battle to take an important bridge and of the fall of Baghdad. Then there were tears when they showed pictures of the Marines who were killed. With the new deployment only a month away, it was a sobering moment. Which of these Marines sitting in their dress blues, dancing with their wives and girlfriends, drinking and sharing stories would not come back? Who would not be at the ball next year? Who would we toast and never see again?

Paul and I danced and drank and tried to forget for a few hours that our time was running out. We spent time with friends, played a few hands of blackjack (and lost), and drank a little more. We didn't go with the groups that left early to venture into Las Vegas. We wanted to get back early to spend some time with Emily. We celebrated Christmas on December 7 that year. It was a Sunday and just a week before Paul was scheduled to leave. We had a small fake tree that sat on a table, and we hung our stockings on the wall. My mom came out, and my dad had sent gifts. Emily didn't care that Christmas was early. She had a blast opening her presents and trying out her new toys. There was a sadness that hung in the air, but with Emily laughing like a loon all day, it was hard to dwell on it.

Before she left the next day, my mom told Paul the same thing she had said to him before he left the last time. "I love you. Don't do anything stupid."

This time around Paul was on the last flight out, December 15, 2003. I told him I didn't want this departure to be like the last time, when he spent the entire last day packing and we hadn't had any time to spend together. This time we had plenty of notice, and there was no reason why he couldn't pack in advance so we could just relax and enjoy each other on the last day. Shows you how little I still knew about my husband. Though I had seen him wait until the last minute to start packing before

Officer Candidate School, the Basic School, field exercises, and the first Iraq deployment, I somehow thought this time would be different. Nope. His unofficial life motto is "If it wasn't for the last minute, I'd never get anything done."

I spent that last week baking, as usual. I put together bags of cookies and truffles for Paul and Andy and more for Paul to give to the communications Marines who were already in Okinawa. Paul also shared them with Sergeant Major Howell who, though he could terrify a unit of Marines with a single glance, had a weakness for chocolate.

By the time December 14 rolled around, I was on edge and irritable. For six months I had been waiting and dreading this day. Paul was leaving the next day. He was going back into combat. His life was going to be in danger. He was going to be gone for seven months. Seven months of being alone with Emily. Seven months of being in Twentynine Palms. Seven months with no one to help if the car breaks down again or if the washing machine explodes. Seven months of taking out the trash, changing diapers, dealing with a sick child, mowing the lawn, and paying the bills. Seven months of praying no one knocks on my door.

As I watched him pack (at midnight the night before his flight), I fought between two emotions. One minute I was sure there was no way I could make it through another deployment. I was going to go crazy, I was going to lose my mind. He couldn't really be leaving. Why was I staying here? Why was I living this life? Then the very next minute I would be frustrated and angry. *Just go already*, I thought. *Just get on the plane and leave, so I can get on with living without you.* The tension of the past six months was catching up with me. I didn't want him to leave, but because there was no way to change it, I just wanted it to be over.

I also wanted Paul to be upset about leaving; I wanted him to be sad and cry and tell me how much he didn't want to go. I knew this was his job, I knew he had to go, but I wanted him to do something that showed me that he wanted to be with Emily and me instead. But Paul keeps those kinds of emotions inside. He just kept packing. I wanted him to tell me he tried to get out of it, even though I knew he'd never do that. I wanted him to feel bad about going, but then again I didn't want him to feel bad.

Mostly, I was just scared.

Fortunately, I knew I wasn't the only wife feeling this way. It was common for all of us wives to get to the point where we just wanted our husbands to leave so we could be done with the planning and the waiting. It was kind of like being nine-months pregnant; you don't look forward to the actual act of giving birth, but you finally get to the point where you're so fed up with being pregnant you just want to be done with it—even if it means pushing a watermelon through an opening the size of a lemon.

By this time Paul was getting into his deployment mindset. His mind was already on the mission. We went through the same sequence of events as the first deployment. Paul put Emily down to bed and spent a long time just holding her and then watching her sleep. I gave him pictures and cookies and pre-addressed envelopes I knew he probably wouldn't use. His plane wasn't leaving until the next afternoon, so we went to bed that night, both nervous and anxious. There wasn't any Marine-going-to-war farewell sex. We just held each other and whispered in the dark, and tried to sleep.

The next day we drove to the bus site only to find out his plane had been delayed three hours. So we drove home—and didn't know what to do with ourselves. Everything was packed, we'd said our big good-byes. I had prepared myself to wave good-bye and drive home without him. Now what were we supposed to do? We waited. We took Emily down to the park and let her play for a while. We had lunch and talked and waited.

Then we drove back down to the pick-up site. We unloaded Paul's bags, and I held Emily as he, the senior officer on the flight, went to get a time of departure. Then he came back. Delayed again. This time the flight wasn't leaving until the next morning. So we loaded everything back in the car and drove home—again.

During the first deployment, when I came home from saying good-bye to Paul at the buses, my mom and I spent some time in the backyard. While we were sitting out there, I saw Steve and Justine rush by on their inline skates. Steve had been scheduled to leave, but his plane had been delayed. I remember being so upset that they got to spend an extra day together. My mom tried to soften the blow by telling me that I only saw them having fun, I wasn't seeing them having to say good-bye over and over again.

And though I understood what she meant, I didn't get it until all those months later when it happened to us.

I don't remember what we did with our bonus day, except that we finally had our Marine-going-to-war farewell sex that night. We had both been so tense and upset the previous night, but this unexpected reprieve made us much more relaxed. I pointed out to Paul only once that this was why it was good to pack ahead of time and not wait until the last minute. It wasn't really an "I told you so"—more of a helpful observation.

The next morning we went through the good-bye routine again. There was no delay this time. We drove to the pick-up site, and Paul dropped off his bags. One of his good friends, Brian, was also on this flight, and his wife and son were there as well. Brian's wife was also named Michelle, and they had a seven-year-old son named Jeremy. Michelle and Jeremy hadn't been living in California during the first deployment, but they had since moved out and were living just a few houses down from us. Michelle was also expecting their second child. Brian was scheduled to transfer to Okinawa and would be coming home from Iraq a few months early, and we all hoped it would be in time for the birth.

As we said our good-byes, Michelle and I stood near each other. She held Jeremy's hand, and I had Emily in my arms. There wasn't much to say as we watched our husbands stow their bags and check in with the buses.

"If you need anything," I said to her. "Don't hesitate to ask, OK?"

"Thanks. You too," she replied. But neither of us was really listening to anything other than the voice in our head that kept reminding us that our husbands were going back to war.

When Paul returned from dropping off his bag, he gave me a kiss and a hug. Then he held Emily for a while. He kissed her while she played with his cover.

"I'll call you as soon as I can," he said and put his arms around me.

"OK. I love you, Marine."

"I love you too."

And still, my husband hated good-byes. So after another hug, he said simply, "Stay here." Then he went to the bus and climbed in.

I thought he was checking his bags or putting stuff away, but he didn't come back.

Brian was still standing with Michelle and Jeremy. He was telling his son to be good and to be the man of the house and help his mother. Then he kissed Michelle and gently rubbed her stomach, saying good-bye to a child he hadn't even met yet. Michelle cried as they hugged and said their good-byes.

I stood there with Emily, watching the tears and kisses going on around me, staring into the darkened windows of the bus. Wasn't Paul coming back? Was that it? No more chances to say, "I love you," no more kisses, no more anything? The remaining Marines started to file into the bus, and I heard the rumble of the engine start. This really was it. I didn't even know where he was on the bus. I couldn't see him so I just waved at the side of the bus as the tears rolled down my face hoping that he'd see me once more before the bus disappeared around the corner. He never even said good-bye.

There was a strange silence that followed after the bus pulled away. Those of us left behind just stood there for a while, each in our own little world. There wasn't anything to say. We had all begun the countdown. One minute down, seven months to go. *Please let him come home safely.*

Slowly we all piled into our minivans and SUVs and sedans and drove back to our quiet houses. As I fastened Emily into her car seat, she pulled on my hair and smiled, totally unaware of what had just happened.

"Well, sweetheart," I said. "Looks like it's just you and me—again."

# Chapter 13

# OKINAWA

M y theory at the start of the second deployment was "It can't be as bad as last time." Nothing could be worse than sending your husband off to war, worrying about chemical weapons and the strength of the Iraqi army, and the uncertainty of not even knowing how long he would be gone. This deployment couldn't be as bad as that. The war was essentially won, we had a definite timetable of seven months, this deployment would be more like peacekeeping, so it would be easier, less stressful, less dangerous. Right? Of course, the point of a theory is to see if it holds up during the first test. My theory failed miserably.

Christmas Day was rotten that year. Paul and I had taken down all the decorations from our early Christmas, and I didn't put them back up, so the house didn't even have a Christmasy feel to it. My mom was flying, my dad and stepmother stayed in northern California, so it was just Emily and me on a desert winter day. Emily didn't know any better—it really was just another day to her. When I couldn't stand being in the house anymore— there was nothing on TV except *Miracle on 34th Street*, *Santa Claus is Coming to Town*, and Christmas specials—I took Emily for a walk. Big, bad idea.

Down every street there were dads out playing with their kids, setting up the new basketball net, teaching their kids to ride their new bikes, and jumping out of the way of the new motorized toy Jeep. Every block made me more miserable. It was a Christmas conspiracy. I took Emily to the park and let her play. Fortunately the park was deserted, so I had plenty of time to sulk and feel sorry for myself.

Paul called that night. He told me about the Christmas party they had had, and he talked to Emily for a while. Truthfully, I couldn't wait for the day to end.

I thought that because I had just gone through it, I would fall into my deployment routine easily this time around. But it didn't happen that way. It was just as hard this time to adjust to Paul being gone. Emily was older, which was both a good thing and a bad thing. She was more active, she was more energetic, she was more opinionated. I had the basic things down—writing letters, sending care packages, jumping on the phone when it rang and hoping that it would be Paul. But for some reason the idea of doing these things every day for seven months was overwhelming. Seven months just seemed so long. I tallied up all the holidays and birthdays and anniversaries that Paul would miss—again. I couldn't even imagine what January would be like, let alone July when he could finally come home. Maybe it was the fact that we had just done this, that this time I knew what it was going to be like and what was in store for me, that made it seem so overwhelming.

From the very beginning this deployment had a different feel, and not in a good way. The guys first went to Okinawa for about six weeks. They were training, picking up gear, getting ready for the move back into Iraq. During their few weeks in Okinawa, our lives back in Twentynine Palms was crazed. All of the wives were trying to get through the days, but a large number of the families back home visited a happy place I like to call "Crisis Land." It's kind of like Disneyland, but the Matterhorn is an emotional roller coaster and the puppets in "It's a Small World" really are out to get you.

It was not the smooth transition we had hoped for, and the whole deployment felt a little off. The mission in Iraq was so different from what it was during the first deployment, and none of us knew what to expect in terms of resistance or danger. That feeling of uncertainty was just too much for many of the wives in the unit. Plus we were all still recovering from the last deployment. For many of us, we had just gotten back into a routine, just become used to having our husbands home again when they left. I suppose it would be like running a marathon and then going out the next day and trying to do it again—except this was an emotional marathon. And so many of us just weren't ready yet.

While Krista and I were trying to deal with our husbands suddenly being gone, I had a toddler to chase after, and Krista had a one-year-old and was pregnant again. At the same time, we were inundated by phone calls from wives and family members. Plus, we were having problems with the rear party (which was being led by Gunnery Sergeant Justice)—or the "remain behind element" as Gunny Justice called it, because, as he said, "This ain't no party." I think Gunny Justice didn't know what to do with the KVs. He seemed to be very good at dealing with Marines, but I don't think he really liked dealing with military wives. Tasks were accomplished, the rear party office

Paul and me sharing our first dance at our wedding reception on May 6, 2000, in San Diego, California.

Paul and me at his commissioning ceremony at the Marine Corps Recruit Depot in San Diego, California, in June 2000.

Paul and me together for the first time following the first deployment at the reunion in May, 2003. Emily is caught between us. *Jennifer Johnston*

Maj. Russell Boyce, his wife, Krista, and their five-month-old son, Kyle, at the reunion in May 2003, following the first deployment. *Jennifer Johnston*

Lynde and her husband, 1st Lieutenant Jay Phillips, at the reunion following the first deployment in May 2003. Jay and Lynde soon left Twentynine Palms and transferred to Norway. *Jennifer Johnston*

Ann Baker, the Key Volunteer Advisor for Three-Four during the first deployment, and her husband Major Matt Baker, the battalion's Executive Officer, at the May 2003 reunion following the first Iraq deployment. Matt later transferred to Marine Corps Community Services and was promoted to Lieutenant Colonel.
*Jennifer Johnston*

Paul, Emily, and me at our early Christmas celebration in December, 2003. Paul left for his second deployment to Iraq only a week later.

Paul stands beside an Iraqi flag at the Haditha police station in the Al-Anbar region of Iraq during his second deployment. *Paul Keener*

1st Lieutenant Cade Walton, his daughter Lynsey, and wife, Julie, at the July 2004 reunion following the second deployment. Cade and Julie left the Marine Corps shortly after to move back to Texas. *Julie Walton*

Emily and me at the reunion in July 2004, following Paul's second deployment to Iraq. Emily is holding the teddy bear Paul brought her from Iraq. *Paul Keener*

Paul and Emily together again at the reunion in July 2004, following his second deployment. Emily had just turned two years old in June. *Michelle Keener*

*(above)* Krista Boyce, Lieutenant Colonel Bryan McCoy, me, and Major Andy Petrucci at the Key Volunteer Appreciation Dinner in July 2004. Lieutenant Colonel McCoy eventually transfered back to Quantico and was promoted to Colonel. Major Petrucci also transferred back to Quantico to work as General Mattis' aide.
*Paul Keener*

*(left)* Krista Boyce and me at the Key Volunteer Appreciation Dinner in July 2004 at the Twentynine Palms Officer's Club. We were reunited a year later when Paul and I moved back to Virginia and bought a house less than a mile from the Boyce's.
*Paul Keener*

Paul and me at a formal dinner event in April 2005, celebrating the return of the 7th Marine Regiment to Twentynine Palms, California. *Julie Walton*

ran smoothly (or so it seemed), but he just wasn't a fan of being the go-to guy for all of the wives, which, truthfully, is a large part of the rear party's job. The tension between him and the wives was illustrated by the fact that we all still called him Gunny Justice, even though he called all of us by our first names. (Some of us called him a few other names, but I won't repeat those here.) During the first deployment we had all been on a first-name basis with Fabian (Staff Sergeant Garcia) and the other rear party Marines—now it was "Gunny Justice."

Our first battle with Gunny Justice was over the newsletter. First, Gunny wanted all the KVs to put their phone numbers in the newsletter so the wives would call us before they called the rear party. Uh, no—not after what happened when our names ended up on the Internet during the first deployment. He also wanted the newsletter to come out quarterly. Krista and I wanted to publish it every month, as has always been done when the battalion deploys. We have wives who need information from the unit, who need to know how to get in touch with the rear party. We had events and meetings scheduled, resources available—that newsletter needed to come out every month. I was not planning on losing that battle, and I am not ashamed to admit that I resorted to fighting dirty.

"I don't see why we need a monthly newsletter," Gunny grumbled—again.

"Well, Gunny, it would be helpful for the wives and the last time I spoke with Andy . . . oh, I mean Major Petrucci, he agreed."

Using the XO's name got me what I wanted. The newsletter came out every month. We compromised on the KV contact info, and my phone number was the only one published. I didn't mind, because once a wife called me I figured out who her Key Volunteer was and I sent the wife to that KV. I also had to write a monthly article, but that wasn't too bad.

Our next test was only three weeks after the Marines left. I got a late night call from one of my KVs with Lima Company.

"Hello?" (OK, it may have sounded more like "Hellumph?")

"Michelle? It's Mary. Did I wake you up?" *More importantly, did you wake my daughter up? But fortunately all was quiet on the monitor.*

"It's OK, Mary. What's up?"

"I'm having a problem with one of my wives."

"What's going on?"

"Well, I've been talking to her for a few days now, and she sounds really upset. It's her first deployment, and she has a new baby and I think she's kind of losing it."

"What do you mean?" Losing it can run anywhere from imagining creative ways to punish your husband for ever joining the Marine Corps to, well, actually punishing your husband for joining the Marine Corps.

"She's been calling over to Okinawa three or four times a day. She's demanding that her husband come home."

"Have you told her about the basic way a deployment runs? What she can expect?" The first deployment is rough on a wife. It might be her first real time on her own and with a new baby everything gets magnified. It's worse if you are thrown into it without any prior preparation. It's a horrible feeling to be tossed into this very different and very strange world of military life without anyone to help you through. Fortunately, the Marine Corps has some great programs for wives to learn about the corps, the way it runs, and the base organizations that are available to help.

"Yeah, but she's really pissed."

"Try getting her over to the LINKS [one of those above-mentioned programs for military spouses to get an introduction to military life]. If she needs someone to talk to, send her over to Marine Corps Community Services to help her find counseling."

"OK, Michelle. Thanks. Sorry to wake you up."

"That's OK, that's what I'm here for." And I went back to sleep.

The next morning I called Gunny Justice at the rear party to let him know that we had an angry wife. Ordinarily I might not have bothered him with it, but because she was calling Okinawa I thought he might want to know. Turns out she had been calling the rear party daily as well wanting to know how she could get her husband to come home.

After talking to Gunny Justice about her, I e-mailed Andy over in Okinawa. My message went something like this:

*Andy:*

*I hope you're doing well and not working too hard. All is well back here. I've got one situation I thought you might want to know about. Sarah White* [not her real name] *has been having some difficulties adjusting to the deployment and she's been calling the KVs, the rear party, and Okinawa every day. She thinks her husband can come home whenever he wants. We're working on it. Just thought you'd want to know.*

*Take care, Michelle*

I got a response that same day; turns out Andy never sleeps.

*Michelle:*

*We're aware of Sarah's calls. It's been brought to the attention of the command over here. Keep me posted.*

*Andy*

OK, now if, as a military wife, you ever do anything that is "brought to the attention of the command," and your husband is not the command—stop doing it! Technically the Marine Corps is not supposed to consider family members and their actions as a reflection on the Marine. But if, let's say, you are calling your husband's command three or four times a day and taking up their time and pulling your husband away from his duties, as in this case, that's not a good thing. My best guess is that Sarah's husband was eventually pulled aside and told to tell his wife to stop calling so often during working hours. My second best guess is that the news did not sit well with Sarah because I got another call from her KV the following night.

"Michelle? It's Mary again."

"Hey Mary, what's up?"

"It's Sarah. She's really upset. She said the company commander yelled at her husband."

*He probably did.* "Well, hopefully she'll start to settle down."

"She says she's going to kill herself."

"What?" *Oh crap!*

"I don't know if she means it or not, but she's crying and . . . Michelle, she has a little baby."

*OK, OK, what do we do? Think Michelle.* "Mary, call her back and tell her we are sending PMO [military police] over to her house."

"PMO? Why?"

"Because she made a suicidal threat and she has a baby in the house. I'm going to call the rear party and have them organize with PMO. I'll be in touch."

Unfortunately, because it was after hours, Gunny Justice wasn't answering his cell phone. Here's my voice-mail message, complete with subtext:

"Gunny Justice, it's Michelle *(answer your phone!)*. Sarah White has just threatened to kill herself, and we need to get PMO over there *(where are you?)*. Call me back as soon as you get this message. I'm going to call PMO and I'll get back to you *(help!)*."

As soon as I hung up, my phone rang again. "Michelle? It's Mary again. I just talked to Sarah. She had called Okinawa again and told her husband she was going to kill herself. He called PMO from there, and they're at her house now."

So I couldn't find Gunny in Twentynine Palms, and Okinawa could send PMO quicker than our rear party? That inspires all kinds of confidence.

"Well, that's good. Who's got the baby?"

"She left it with her neighbor who is another of my wives. I think Sarah's going to the hospital."

"That's probably where she needs to go. Thanks, Mary."

I will freely admit that I felt way out of my element on this one. I was worried for Sarah and her baby. I didn't know the next step to take, and I had a sudden sinking feeling that I was supposed to be the one in charge. I really wanted someone to tell me what to do next. I tried calling Gunny again after Sarah was taken to the hospital and still got no answer. So I did what any good Marine would do—I went over his head.

*Andy:*

*Quick update on Sarah White. She called her husband in Okinawa and made a suicidal threat. He contacted Twentynine Palms PMO, and they went to her house and have taken her to the hospital. Her baby is with a neighbor. Thought you'd like to be in the loop on this one. Gunny Justice was nowhere to be found, so I left the info on his voicemail.*

*Take care, Michelle*

Andy's response:

*Michelle:*

*Thank you for the information. It's time for the KVs to step back from this situation and let the command take over. Thanks for all your work with Sarah. I'll send Mary an e-mail as well.*

*Andy*

And that was that. I was officially out of the loop. Sarah went to the hospital and then left Twentynine Palms to go stay with her family. We would come to find out later that she had a history of depression and mental illness. Her husband stayed with the battalion and finished the deployment. It was a terrible thing for Sarah to go through, and it was a stressful introduction to the deployment for Krista and me. It did result in a good long talk between Gunny Justice and me, and in the end that helped.

Of course, my theory that this deployment wouldn't be too bad was tested again while the guys were still in Okinawa. I had another wife from Lima Company call me. Betsy (not her real name) wasn't getting along with Mary, and she wanted to talk to me instead. OK, no big deal—I didn't mind. Well, turned out that Betsy had developed a noncancerous form of leukemia. Crisis number two. I could even hear the Crisis Land ride announcement: "Welcome to Mr. Toad's medical emergency. Please keep your hands and feet inside the car until all blood tests known to man have been finished."

Betsy and I spoke every day for nearly two weeks. Poor Betsy had test after test done. She had to drive to Palm Springs for everything, because our base hospital wasn't equipped for what she was dealing with. There were e-mails back and forth between Andy and me trying to decide if her husband had to come home or not. Betsy vacillated between wanting her husband home with her and wanting him to be able to do his job. In the end she was able to receive treatment in Palm Springs and make a good recovery; her husband stayed with Three-Four and went to Iraq. (Nearly two years later, Betsy was expecting their first baby when her husband was sent back to Iraq. She asked me to be her labor coach. I was able to be there for the birth and even send the new daddy the first pictures of his baby girl. There are some bonds of friendship that can never be broken.)

It was also during this deployment that I met Julie Walton. It seemed innocent enough: a simple introduction, nice to meet you, and all that. Turns out she and I would form a friendship that would last for years, Even to the strangely telepathic point where once we had both left Twentynine Palms, we both got pregnant with our second children at the same time—even shared the same due date!

Julie is the tiniest woman you have ever seen. Small, blonde, skinny (and I still like her!), and as Texas as they come. She likes her pedicures, wine, and designer purses. She owns more shoes than Sarah Jessica Parker, and she adores her husband, Cade.

While the battalion was still in Okinawa, Julie made a trip out there to celebrate Cade's thirtieth birthday. We were all ridiculously green with envy and dogged her for every last detail about our husbands. I loved hearing about the time she was able to spend with Paul and the pictures she gave to me of him, but in the very dark recesses of my mind was a jealousy over the fact that she got to see my husband and I didn't. Even worse was the fear that if he didn't come home, my last memory of him would be of saying good-bye and the way he looked getting into the bus, but her last memory of him would be of him smiling and laughing at the birthday party in the Officer's Club. I knew it was a twisted thought, but it was there. Just as all the other twisted thoughts were there. *What if he dies?*

*What if he's paralyzed? What if he runs off with some Iraqi woman?* (Not a frequent thought, but still there.) None of those thoughts are normal married-life stuff. But no one ever said military life was normal. Besides, as Julie would often say, normal is boring. Oh, and she would know—did I mention she's a psychologist?

# Chapter 14

# LIFE GOES ON

A bout a month or so into the deployment, a strange thing happened. Everybody calmed down. The holidays were over, our husbands had been gone for over a month, and we all started to fall into that deployment rhythm again. Just like the first deployment, it took time to adjust to having your husband/partner/handyman/mechanic suddenly gone. There had been so much anger and tension leading up to the deployment, and it finally started to give way to acceptance.

It was as if in those months between the time when the battalion returned from Iraq in May and left again in December, we were all fighting against the reality of a second deployment. So many of us had comforted ourselves with the knowledge that our husbands might be gone, but at least they would be safe in Okinawa. Then when that comfort was taken away from us and we were faced with the worry and stress of Iraq a second time, it all boiled over. That's my personal theory as to why the first few weeks of the deployment were so chaotic: holidays (which are usually enough to make you nuts) and anger.

Between the deployments, when Paul had to go into the field for a week or two, I would get so angry and frustrated, and I would take it out on him. I think somewhere in the back of my mind I kept thinking that if I was really angry and really made my feelings clear—"I'm pissed off about this, and I don't want you to go"—then somehow he would look at me and say, "Oh, sorry, dear, I didn't know this was so tough on you. Let me call my CO and tell him I can't attend the training exercise." And I knew that would never happen, I didn't actually expect it to happen, but I was just so upset that he wasn't doing anything at all to stop it. But of course, Paul got to the acceptance stage much quicker than I did. He knew his job, what was expected of him, and what he couldn't change. Going to the field for two weeks—roger that, sir. Going to Okinawa—OK, sir. Going back to Iraq—good to go, sir, when do I leave?

But because this wasn't my job or my career and truthfully didn't have anything to do with me, I was still feeling like excess baggage—just along for the ride. It may be presumptuous of me, but I choose to believe that I'm not the only military wife to feel this way. Paul gives me as much input as he can as to where we transfer and what kind of job he takes, but in the end there's really not much I can do about any of it. The Marine Corps is in charge, and Paul has a duty to follow his orders. All I can do is follow along. That's kind of a rotten thing for an independent woman to be faced with.

It was the same thing with the second deployment. Yes, I was upset. No, I didn't want him to go. No, I didn't want to be a single mother for another seven months. And yes, I probably did have my bitchy days before he left because I was mad and there was no one else to blame. Once again, kind of a rotten thing, but it comes with the territory. For all of the benefits of military life, there is always the possibility of war and the possibility that we will be called on to make sacrifices. Just like the first deployment, after a month or two we all began to settle into our routines. I got used to Paul being gone. I remembered to take the trash to the curb on Thursday nights, and I knew how to fix a blown fuse. Not only did I mow the lawn, but I aerated, seeded, and fertilized it as well. I had more time to myself again, so I was able to read a book or watch a chick flick without Paul whining about it. My house was spotless again. I didn't like the fact that Paul was gone, I hated the fact that he was in danger, and I still had my days where I hated the Marine Corps and the whole idea of deployments. And I still had nights where I cried in the shower so Emily wouldn't hear me. But as each day went by, I grew less angry and more comfortable being on my own again.

By the time the battalion moved from Okinawa to Iraq, the majority of the wives back home had moved from resentment to acceptance. The craziness of the first few weeks eased up and gave us all some room to relax. We still got crisis calls and crazy calls and middle-of-the-night breakdown calls, but everyone was definitely calming down. Maybe it had to do with the fact that with our husbands in Iraq, our priorities were shifting again. Most of our energy was going once again to worrying for our husbands' safety or to sending care packages or to waiting. All those things take a lot of energy, and at the end of the day there's not a lot leftover to fuel anger over something you know you can't change.

In February 2004, we had our first big get-together for the families of Three-Four. We planned a day of bowling and pizza at the base bowling alley. It was controlled chaos, but it was fun. We had a pretty good turnout, and it was nice to see everyone together again. So many of the wives had disappeared during those months between the deployments. Everyone had wanted to spend as much time with their husbands as possible, and there hadn't been a lot of socializing going on, so it was good to see wives and their children talking and laughing again.

We had more pizza than the battalion could have eaten, and bowling was free. By this time Emily wasn't just walking, she was running, so I was running too. She was fascinated by the pins and kept trying to run down the bowling lanes. All I could imagine was Emily being squashed by a bowling ball, so I had to keep grabbing her. I spent the entire day with one eye on the women at the event and one eye on her—it's a wonder I'm not permanently cross-eyed.

We didn't have another event scheduled until March, but I was forming an idea for another way to help ease the stress of the wives of deployed Marines. And I knew just who to pester to make it happen.

"Hi, Matt. It's Michelle Keener. How are you?" Major Matt Baker, our former XO, had transferred over to Marine Corps Community Services. He was one of the guys in charge of all the base programs. And once we had an in over there, Krista and I kept him hopping. Fortunately he still had a soft spot for his old unit, so he was always receptive to our needs/wants/ideas/begging.

"Hi, Michelle. I'm good, thanks. How's Paul?"

"He's fine. They've moved over to Iraq now, so he's been busy."

"I know how that goes. What can I do for you?"

"Well," *OK, here goes.* "I have an idea for a new base program, and I don't know how to make it happen."

There was a pause on the other end of the line. I could even hear him thinking, *Oh God, what could she want now?* "OK, what is it?"

"I'd like to get some child care set up at the gyms so the wives can work out."

More silence. "That's a great idea. But I'm not sure that we can do it."

"Why not?" *And of course it's a great idea!* At one of our information briefs before the Marines deployed, an MCCS speaker was giving a talk on the signs of child abuse. His experience with military services had led him to believe that there was a rise in cases of child abuse during deployments. He wanted to make sure we all knew about the resources available to us to prevent us from getting to that level of anger. While I would never condone child abuse, having gone through a deployment, I could see how frustration, burn out, exhaustion, and lack of help can build up to dangerous levels. So when I began to think of my child care at the gym idea, I tried to present it as a way to provide some much needed stress relief and time away from the kids for the wives on base.

"Well, the Child Development Center is in charge of all child care on base, and I don't think they can approve a room for watching the kids at the gyms."

A quick explanation here: the Child Development Center (CDC) is our base child-care center. However, I like to call them the child-care overlords. They insist on having their fingers in every aspect of child care. If you want a sitter for your family event or meeting, you have to go through the CDC. The good news is that their monopoly means that the child care that does get provided is high quality. The bad news is that there are no other options. And I know it's not like this on every base. Quantico has a child-care co-op at the base gym. Which of course I mentioned to Major Baker.

"Yeah, I know they do, but I don't think we can go that way. Our CDC is very strict."

*Strict? More like fanatical.* "But Matt, this is a program that would really help alleviate some of the stress on wives during the deployment. It would give them an outlet, some time away from their children, some time to devote to themselves. Seven months is a long time to never get a break."

More silence. I knew he was considering it. "Let me see what I can do."

*Yippee!* "Thank you, Matt. I knew we could count on you."

It took over a month and a series of e-mails, phone calls, and starts and stops, but we made progress. Sure enough, the CDC wouldn't provide child care at the gym, but they did agree to provide someone to watch the children at the community center on base. It wasn't much, but it was a start. MCCS began to offer aerobics classes at the center, and they moved some cardio equipment into another room at the center. We had it for only a few hours a day, but I was thrilled to have something else started for the wives on base. That's my own personal crusade. If the

Marine Corps is going to take my husband away for months at a time, the least it can do is offer me some helpful programs so I don't lose my mind.

I was back to writing Paul every day (and still he never wrote back) and sending care packages. But it was during this deployment that the post office decided to throw us wives a curve ball. They changed their requirements for filling out the customs forms that had to be attached to each package going overseas. In the past they were pretty lenient on the way we listed the contents of each package. A general "snacks" or "toiletries" would be enough and off the package went to Iraq. But, alas, no more. Now we had to list each and every item in the box. You couldn't just list "toothbrushes and toothpaste." It had to be how many toothbrushes, how much toothpaste. It was nuts. And what made it worse was the fact that our post office on base began hiding the custom forms. Before the customs forms were just out with all the other colored forms in the little boxes; now they were keeping them behind the desk. You had to wait in line, ask for the form, go to the little table with the chained pens to fill out the form (while lugging your care package and children), remember every item you put in the box (which was now thoroughly sealed with clear packing tape), and then get back in line to finally mail the box (that by this time you weren't sure you even wanted to send anymore). That's how much we loved our husbands!

I did this only once, and then I came up with a plan. A devious and brilliant plan—I called my mom. My mom went to the post office by her house in Palm Springs, where they still had the customs forms out in plain view, and helped herself to every form that was there. She kept a few and gave me the rest. So yes, I was hoarding customs forms. I kept them hidden in a drawer in my kitchen, and I would furtively pass them out to wives I knew who were getting ready to send a care package. I couldn't do anything about the rule of listing every item, but at least I wasn't waiting in line twice anymore. Only once did the guy working at the post office ever question how I got my form. I just smiled and said I must have had an extra one (or fifty) lying around.

Not much changed in terms of the things Paul wanted in his care packages this time around. More raspberry frosted Pop-Tarts, less beef jerky (actually, no beef jerky). Powdered Gatorade was good, naked pictures of me would be better (yeah, right). Also during this deployment my aunt changed from the toilet paper fairy to the coffee fairy. You may remember that my husband's two greatest weaknesses are cigars and Starbucks. Well my aunt is an e-Bay pro, and she bought up every ounce of Starbucks coffee to be found and sent it to Paul. And not just any coffee—it couldn't be the house blend or some other normal flavor—he wanted Christmas blend (in April) or raspberry cream. Paul also received a French press from one of my mom's friends who lives in London. The first day my manly Marine husband walked into the chow hall carrying his French press and raspberry-flavored coffee, he was laughed at and teased. The second day he was quietly approached and sniffed. By the third day there was a line forming to share his frou-frou coffee. My husband is very secure in his masculinity, raspberry coffee and all.

So between my work with the KVs, bugging Major Baker for new base programs for the wives left on base, and subverting the base post office, I managed to keep myself busy. And yet, because I am apparently incapable of sitting still for too long, I also found a few new hobbies. I was finally drawn into the scrapbooking obsession that seems to surround military life. I'm bad at it, but I try. I also discovered my favorite hobby during this deployment: getting annoyed at celebrities.

In the months following the first deployment and the famous pulling down of the statue in Baghdad, the media had been slowly but surely turning away from supporting the war effort. During the first deployment we saw red, white, and blue everywhere. News reporters wore flag pins, banners hung in the studios, the *American Idol* contestants sang "God Bless the U.S.A." on national TV. (Yes, I watched *American Idol*, and, yes, I cried my eyes out.) But this time around it was different. Now every time I turned on the television there was some celebrity talking about how wrong the war is and how President Bush lied to us, blah, blah, blah. . . . To these shallow, know-it-all celebrities who patronize our troops by insisting they come home: Since when was International Politics a course at the Actor's Studio? You might have an opinion, but so do those of us who aren't surrounded by bootlicking entertainment reporters. The freedom to express it is precisely what my husband and my friends are fighting for. Yes, President Bush is a Republican, and that automatically makes everything he does wrong by most Hollywood standards, but stop exploiting my husband to criticize the policies of a president you don't like.

Let me tell you how to support your troops. During the second Iraq deployment we had a family event for all the battalions in 7th Marine Regiment. Gunny Justice did most of the planning, and I got there bright and early with Emily in tow to help set up. When I pulled into the parking lot, I noticed a big, bearded biker heading around the back of the community center. Now that's not a sight you often see on base, so I got Emily out of her car seat, grabbed my bags, and went inside. I was immediately greeted by a pack of bikers. Three or four burly, muscled men with long gray beards, leather pants, and black vests.

"Can I help you, ma'am?" asked one man wearing a "Bikers for Jesus" shirt.

"No, I'm good. Thanks." Then I scooped up Emily and hurried back to the room we reserved for the event, convinced that we were being invaded by Hell's Angels. I found Elizabeth Tucker there helping set up table after table filled with toys.

"Elizabeth, what is going on? There's a motorcycle gang on base."

"Oh, you've probably met the guys who donated everything."

*Uh, OK. Guess I feel stupid now.* "The bikers donated all this stuff?"

"Yeah. Can you believe it?" She was grinning from ear to ear. "You haven't even seen everything yet."

As I wandered around the room I saw that this group of bikers from Los Angeles had donated over a thousand toys for children of deployed Marines and sailors. Then they brought in a truckload of nonperishable food for the families to take home. Every one of us could have fed our children for a week on the food they had given us. When I stood dumbfounded in front of the tables loaded with food, two women approached me.

"Can we pack some bags for you?" They offered. "What would you and your daughter like?" I could barely speak because of the lump that formed in my throat. These men and women had brought us food. I just couldn't get over that. For all the talk about supporting our troops and everything we as families went through, these people thought of something so precious as bringing our children toys and giving us food. It seemed so small, but it wasn't. It was one less thing we had to worry about, and I was so touched by the gesture that I gave them both a big hug; of course when Emily saw that she had to hug them too.

Those were the people who truly supported us during the deployments. Not the celebrities who thought they were doing me a favor by saying my husband wanted to come home. You think I don't know that? You think I don't know that every day he's gone is one more day he's missing his daughter's life? You think I don't know that every day he's gone is one more day he might be killed?

"I'm not a president, but I play one on TV" doesn't make you right. It only gives you a microphone that I don't have. And even though I may not be on TV and I may not have a record deal and I may not be a movie star, I have an opinion too—stop talking about your support for my husband. If you really want to support my husband, stop damaging his morale. Stop criticizing what he's fighting for, stop making him feel like his friends have died for nothing. Stop going on TV and telling the wives and children of the men and women who are in harms way that our loved ones are killing innocent people and that their sacrifices have no meaning. Instead of trying to "support the troops" by criticizing the government, try sending a check to the military wife left behind who receives food stamps because her husband is a private and he doesn't make enough money to feed his family. But still he puts his life on the line because that's his duty.

Yes, I'm on another soapbox, and I'm almost done. I'm the last person to tell anyone not to express an opinion even if I don't agree with it. If you're against the war, fine, good for you—that's your right. That's the beauty of our country: freedom of speech and expression, and thank God for it. But can we please give just a bit of thought to the people who have to listen to our opinions? How can it possibly help our troops and their families to see people that they admire and respect going on TV and denigrating everything they're going through? I don't care if you're opposed to the war, and I don't care if you want to go on TV and engage in some thoughtful debate. But don't use my husband as your excuse to go on TV and bash the president. My husband knows what he's fighting for, and so do I. If you really want to support my husband, send him a care package and shut up.

OK, now I'm done.

## Chapter 15

# DIDN'T WE ALREADY WIN THE WAR

It's very hard, impossible actually, not to compare these two Iraq deployments. They came so close together, and most of us in Three-Four went through both of them. The first deployment was like a whirlwind. From the twenty-four-hour notice that they were leaving to the race across Iraq to the victory in Baghdad, it just flew by. The second deployment was different right from the start. Not just the initial series of minor and major emergencies that plagued the wives, but the whole feel of the deployment. The media had largely turned against the war; people were protesting, calling for troops to pull out of Iraq. It seemed like the war ended when the statue came down, so this second deployment just felt strange from the start.

Our Marines left Okinawa in late January 2004 and went to the Al-Anbar province in Western Iraq. They were stationed at a dam in a town called Haditha. They had an actual building to live in, showers that usually worked, and hot meals twice a day—it sounded pretty good. Until we all began to realize that the war wasn't over, it had just changed forms. Instead of the tremendous force moving across Iraq, our Marines were standing their ground and defending themselves and their area against terrorists. We all learned pretty quickly that IED stands for improvised explosive device and that military convoys were constantly under attack. Just as our husbands were fighting an enemy they couldn't always see, we were struggling with a fear of the unknown.

During the first deployment we knew who our husbands were fighting: the Iraqi army. That knowledge conjured up images of great battles between two clearly defined teams. There would be a winner and a loser, and the bad guys were easy to spot. Not so this time around. Now the bad guys were being sneaky. They were planting explosives and just waiting for a Marine truck or vehicle to run it over. They were staging ambushes and infiltrating the civilian population. That fact made for much more uncertainty and uneasiness for the Marines and for those of us back home. It felt like the knock on the door could come at any moment.

In February I actually did get a knock on the door. It was about 7 a.m. and I was still asleep. I heard the doorbell ring, and I was instantly awake. I glanced at the clock, and my heart was hammering so loudly it echoed in my head. *Is this it?* I jumped out of bed and put on my robe. My stomach was in knots, and my throat was so tight I couldn't even swallow. My thoughts were racing over all the information I had about the battalion and where they were, what they were doing. Paul was at the dam, he had to be at the dam. How could he be injured? Or worse?

Then there was a knock at the door. I walked down the hallway from my bedroom. *Please God no. You can't do this, You can't do it. Please, please no.* By the time I got to the front door my hands were shaking and I was convinced that Gunny Justice would be on the other side of the door in his dress blues. I put my hand on the door handle, but it didn't open. I had to force myself to open the door. *God help me.*

When I opened the door, I laughed. The UPS guy was standing there with a big box. I couldn't even speak when

I signed for the stupid package. He must have thought I was insane, standing there in a robe, my hair a tangled mess, giggling like a fool. When I shut the door, I slumped to the floor and cried. I had been absolutely convinced that my time had come. I knew it when I was walking down the hallway, when my hand was on the doorknob. But, it hadn't come. Paul was alive. And I had killed him in my mind. I cried out of relief that he was alive, but I also cried because I felt like I had betrayed him. I had been ready to deal with his death. I felt rotten. How could I be so prepared for that to happen? How could I be a good and loving wife and still be ready at any moment to hear that I was a widow?

That was one of those days. Before my daughter woke up, I sat on the floor and hated my life. This was not normal. Normal people did not live this way. Normal married life did not revolve around deployments and war and waiting for bad news. I was in a bad mood all day. Later that day, Emily was crying over something I can't remember now, and I was so angry and frustrated that I grabbed one of her toys off the floor and threw it across the room. It hit the closet door and left a nice scuff mark, which I left on the door for the rest of the deployment. Poor Emily. Her eyes got wide, and she just stared at me in shock. I was ready to scream. I didn't, but I sure wanted to.

I know I wasn't the only wife to go through those ups and downs and when I told Krista about the UPS delivery, she said I should have decked the guy. But there were days when I just felt so alone in it. Even though my neighbors were in the same situation, some days it just felt like I was the only one freaking out. Many months later, Krista told me how much she admired the strength I had shown during the deployments, the fact that I always looked so calm and pulled together. I guess all those acting classes finally paid off. It meant so much for her to say that to me, but what I remember is throwing that toy across the room because I was ready to give up.

But I got through that day. And the next one. In retrospect it sounds a little bit like Alcoholics Anonymous: one day at a time. Maybe that's what we all needed—a WA group: Wives Anonymous; "Hello, my name is Michelle, and I'm a Marine wife," I guess we did have that. We had each other. We had our phone calls and our visits and our venting sessions. Once, when Jennifer was having a bad day, she mentioned a phone call from Tony where they had argued over something for the house. Jennifer's statement to all of us when she related the story had been, "It's *my* house. He doesn't really live here anyway." I've always remembered that comment because it was just so perfect and so true. Paul and I joked that when it was time for us to leave Twentynine Palms I would have been there for three years and he would have been there for eighteen months.

It didn't help any of us in the KVN that so many of our wives were frustrated and tense. The Marines were sitting at a dam! Why couldn't they call more? Why couldn't they come home sooner? Why? Why? Why? Krista once remarked to me that when the unit goes on a "normal" deployment like to Okinawa, wives tend to get all testy and frustrated and complain. But when the guys go to war, everyone gets their priorities in line. What we had was a strange combination of the two. Yes, they were in harm's way, but the deployment was starting to feel normal, as though the guys were just in Okinawa. We started to get some nasty complaints and phone calls from the wives. My position as KV coordinator was both a blessing and a curse. I didn't have to field the everyday calls, but I did have to handle the problem calls. No one ever said, "Wow, that's great news, let me have you call Michelle." Oh no, I got, "Wow, that is terrible, and I don't know how to handle it, so let me give you Michelle's phone number."

At one of our monthly KVN meetings, I tried to figure out a way to address all the issues we had been having with wives in the unit and how frustrating and upsetting it could be for all of us.

"I know it can be difficult to deal with an angry wife," I began and immediately heads were nodding up and down. "I also know that each one of you is having to deal with missing your husband and all the worry you're experiencing. I'm going through that too." *Now, how to make this a pep talk?* "All we can do is just keep getting through one day at a time. Know that you can call me whenever you need to." *Still not feeling very peppy.* "We all need to just . . . "

"Keep swimming?" Venus spoke up from the front row.

"Excuse me?" *Did she say swimming? Uh-oh, I may be losing one.* "What do you mean?"

"Just keep swimming. You know, *Finding Nemo?*" Then she started to sing. "Just keep swimming, just keep swimming, swimming, swimming . . ." And everyone started to laugh. Pep talk achieved!

"That's it!" I managed to say between fits of laughter. "We all need to just keep swimming." From that day on I made "just keep swimming" my unofficial deployment motto.

After the initial series of emergencies happened at the beginning of the deployment, it was relatively quiet for a time. Then we had one last incident with a wife. Jennifer Shealy was the wife of one of Paul's communication Marines. I had spoken with her a number of times; she had three children, and her husband was assigned as Lieutenant Colonel McCoy's driver. One day I received a phone call from one of the KVs.

"Michelle, it's Brandy." Brandy Parkin was one of our Weapons Company volunteers. "I thought you should know that there's an ambulance and PMO outside the house of one of the Three-Four wives."

Wow. Not what I was expecting when I answered the phone. "Who is it?"

"Jennifer Shealy. I think she's in H&S."

"Yeah, I know her." I immediately felt protective of her because not only was she a Three-Four wife, but also because her husband was one of Paul's Marines. "What's going on?"

"I'm not sure, but I thought you'd want to know."

"I sure do. Thanks for the heads up, Brandy."

So I hang up and immediately call Gunny Justice.

"Gunny, it's Michelle. There's an ambulance and PMO at Jennifer Shealy's house. Have they contacted you yet?" Ordinarily, because Jennifer's husband is deployed, the hospital or PMO would notify the rear party of what's happened.

"No, I haven't heard anything yet." I can tell Gunny is annoyed. He doesn't like to be the last to know anything.

"Gunny, she's got three kids."

"OK, I'll call you when I hear something." Click.

So I waited and waited until we got some word on what had happened. Jennifer had had a medical emergency, and a neighbor had called 911. She was taken to the hospital and admitted for a few days. Her children (and here's where I get irritated) were taken into foster care because there was no family around and because Jennifer hadn't gotten a "special power of attorney to designate a caregiver." Her neighbor had children of her own and wasn't prepared to care for an additional three children for an indefinite period of time.

Oh, I was mad! We are supposed to have emergency child care on base to fill in for such a situation. I immediately called Major Baker over at Marine Corps Community Services. I explained the situation to him and wanted to know why the emergency child-care program hadn't been used.

"PMO never called the child-care contact, and there was no one else available to watch the kids," he replied once he had asked around.

E-mails were racing between myself and the XO and the rear party. I actually got a phone call over it.

"Michelle? It's Andy."

"Andy who?"

"Uh, Andy Petrucci."

"Oh! Where are you?"

"Um . . . Iraq."

"Oh, right, of course . . . why are you calling me?"

"What's going on with Shealy's family?"

I gave him all the information I had, and the command decided that Lance Corporal Shealy would be sent home immediately to help his wife and kids. When he got back, there was a legal issue about getting the kids out of foster care, and I had a number of follow-up calls and e-mails from the XO to make sure all was going well. Apparently Lieutenant Colonel McCoy really liked Shealy and wanted to make sure that he was going to be taken care of back home. The good news is that the kids finally came home, and Lance Corporal Shealy got to stay behind as a member of the rear party. On more than one occasion he showed up as a rear party representative at our family events.

Small emergencies aside, we were getting through the deployment relatively well. The bad news is that our sense of "it's a normal deployment" didn't last long. While our guys were at Haditha doing their job to quell insurgency activity in western Iraq, there was a battle brewing in Fallujah. Most of us had seen the news coverage of the desecration of the bodies of American civilian contractors in Fallujah, and we were thankful our husbands were far away from that mess. Then came the news.

Three-Four was going to Fallujah.

The information filtered down slowly at first. *I'm sorry, could you repeat that?* No, you heard it right the first time—our Marines were on their way to Fallujah. First there were rumors passed on from husbands calling home. Then there were rumblings from the rear party. Then I had a phone call from Paul.

"Hey, honey, I wanted to tell you that we're going on the move. I might not be able to call for a while."

"Where are you going?" I asked, even though I was pretty sure I already knew.

"You know I can't tell you that over the phone." Which means bad news.

"I've been hearing rumors. Are they true?" Back to our espionage code talk.

"Probably."

"Does it begin with F?" There's a long pause over the phone. For a moment I think we've been disconnected again, but I can hear him breathing. "Never mind," I say. "I know what that means."

"I'll call you when I can, but I don't know when that will be."

"You know you could write a letter."

He laughed. "Yeah, right."

"Be safe. It looks nasty down there."

"Wait until they see us." He paused again. "I love you, Michelle." Now I know it's serious because he never calls me Michelle—it's always honey or sweetheart. So I do my job and keep it together.

"I love you too, Marine." Paul then talked to Emily for a few minutes. I checked on the phone when she stopped talking, and Paul wasn't there anymore—the connection was lost. Not long after that I got a confirmation e-mail from the XO.

*Michelle: The Batallion is on the move. We are heading to Fallujah to aid in the fight for the city. Andy*

# Chapter 16

# THE XO

Now may be a good time to devote some pages to Major Andy Petrucci, the executive officer for Three-Four during the second OIF deployment. Andy came on board following Major Matt Baker. We all had felt a little spoiled with Matt as the XO and the family readiness officer because he had been so involved with the KVN. So when Major Petrucci arrived at the battalion we were a little skeptical. Because I was the KV coordinator, Andy would be my primary contact person. As it would turn out, he became my best buddy for the deployment. I harassed him, badgered him for information, dropped all my biggest problems in his lap and expected him to fix them, and was generally a pain in his Marine Corps' rear end. What's not to love about that?

I had Andy's e-mail address not only memorized, but I could also probably type it with my eyes closed. Andy and I had a number of personality quirks in common that made it easy for us to communicate—we're both control freaks who think sarcasm is a virtue. The funny thing is, we barely saw each other. We only worked together for a few months between the time he arrived and when the battalion deployed, but through the grace of e-mail we were in constant contact.

Just before the second deployment, I asked Andy how much information he wanted from me. Did he want only the most important issues sent to him, or did he want the smallest details of life with the wives back in Twentynine Palms? Well, being the control freak that he is, he wanted all the details. And that's exactly what he got. I, of course, never failed to remind him that he asked for it.

Andy was a great source of information for those of us back home. He would send the KVs regular e-mail updates on the battalion, and he always let every KV know that we could go straight to him with questions or concerns. And because we weren't always getting what we wanted from the rear party, having Andy as our personal answer man really helped. (Well, it helped us. It probably just gave him more work to do.) But we truly would have been lost without him during that second deployment.

I definitely kept Andy in the loop on what was going on in Twentynine Palms. More than once I mentioned to Paul that I was afraid I was being too much of a pest and that Andy was probably just too polite to tell me to shut up. Paul explained that the XO was the type of guy who preferred too much information to too little. So he got everything. Andy also had my home and cell phone numbers with him in Okinawa and Iraq. He made it a habit to call my cell phone during our KVN meetings so he could "be there" to answer questions. Now keep in mind that when we had a meeting at six or seven in the evening in California, he would be calling at 5 a.m. Iraq time. That is going above and beyond the call of duty.

I was in such constant contact with the XO that it became a joke. Paul called me once and told me about a conversation he had had with the XO.

"Morning, sir. Are you busy?" Paul asked him.

"No," Andy replied. "Just e-mailing your wife." Now that's not a response you expect to hear very often.

At one of my KV meetings I announced to the group that Andy would be calling my cell phone at some point so we could pass on our questions to him. Then one of my brand-new KVs spoke up.

"Andy is your husband, right?" *Wow*, I thought, *do I talk to him that much?*

"No," I replied. "I'm married to the communications officer."

"Oh," she said with some confusion. "Who's that?" Fortunately, my real husband has a great sense of humor and found all of this very funny.

As I began working with Andy, I started out with polite, to-the-point e-mails. These quickly degenerated to joking and sarcastic one-liners. Here is the first e-mail I sent him, just after I took over as the KV coordinator and when I was trying to track down the new rosters listing all of the Three-Four wives we needed to contact.

*September 11, 2003*

*Andy,*

*Sorry you missed my first e-mail . . . I had the wrong email address. We'll get it corrected on our next KVN list. I was hoping you and the chaplain could generate an HS Co. married roster for us.*

*Krista also said you need the e-mail distribution list for the KVs. I don't have it on my computer anymore, but I'll try to track one down to forward to you. Thanks for all your help. Take care.*

*Michelle*

And his response:

*September 12, 2003*

*Michelle,*

*Here's what we found. We are currently in the process of cleaning it up so it is a little more user friendly and easier to read. Please let me know if the information is wrong when the ladies start making phone calls so I can administer the appropriate beatings to the appropriate personnel.*

*Thanks,*

*Andy*

As we got to know each other better, I figured out that the XO likes to be entertained in his e-mails.

*October 8, 2003*

*Andy,*

*We are all set to hold our monthly meeting next Wednesday at 6:30 . . . oh . . . let me translate for you . . . we're meeting 15 Oct at 1830 (impressive huh?).*

*Hope you are doing well, getting sleep, and wearing sunscreen. Take care.*

*Michelle*

Another running joke in the battalion became the fact that if I ever joined the Marine Corps (yeah, we're all holding our breath for that one) my call sign should be "yes, dear." When the Marines were out in the field at Twentynine Palms and especially when they crossed back to Iraq, I became the sunscreen Nazi. The majority of Paul's care packages had at least one bottle of sunscreen, SPF 1000 (or whatever the highest number they make is). Most of my e-mails to various Marines during the deployment—Paul, Andy, Lieutenant Colonel McCoy, even the chaplain— usually ended with some sort of nagging about wearing sunscreen or eating well or getting enough rest. The general response: "Yes, dear." What can I say? I'm a mom.

As the deployment date came closer, a nasty rumor began to fly. Would the battalion be extended in Iraq? There were concerns that the seven-month deployment didn't mean two months in Okinawa plus five months in Iraq—it actually meant that the Marines had to be in Iraq for seven months. That would translate to our husbands not coming home until October or November—not what wives wanted to hear. So when I stared getting calls about the possibility of Three-Four being deployed longer than seven months, I figured the XO should suffer for it too.

*December 2, 2003*

*Andy,*

*As far as Iraq info . . . all I need right now is an official line to give to the KVs and to the wives. We'll take the rest of the info as it comes.*

*Thanks for everything. Hope you find time to eat and sleep!*

*Michelle*

Turns out, the rumor was being spread by the Marines (as usual). There is always a chance that the deployement will be extended beyond its scheduled end. During the first Iraq deployment, this happened to another Twentynine Palms unit, 2nd Battalion, 7th Marines, which had been in the midst of a routine six-month deployment to Okinawa when Marines were sent to Iraq. Well, because every other battalion in Twentynine Palms was sent to Iraq, there was no one to relieve Two-Seven in Okinawa. They ended up spending ten months over there. With that memory fresh in all of our minds, none of us wanted to face the possibility of our guys being extended and spending even more time in a combat zone. It was a fear and a rumor that we would have to deal with throughout the deployment.

Andy was great at sending the KVs e-mail updates on the battalion's movements. He was the first person to let us know that everyone had arrived safely in Okinawa and that they were ready to begin training. I learned early on that I had to be careful what I wrote to Andy. If I casually mentioned a problem we were having, he would take that as a sign to go to battle for us. Such a guy! Sometimes I was just giving him an update and wasn't really expecting his help, but being a man, and a Marine on top of it, he usually jumped right in.

Andy took his responsibility to the wives of the battalion very seriously. If it was in his power to do something for us, he would do it. It helped all of us to know that the guys who were in charge of our husbands, the guys who were giving the orders, were willing to listen to us and help if they could. Sometimes there was nothing that could be done. There were times when a Marine just couldn't be sent home or couldn't come in from the field. But sometimes, they would really go to bat for us.

Early on in the deployment when the unit was still in Okinawa, we had one wife who unfortunately suffered a miscarriage. Her husband was able to come home for ten days to be with her. Months later, when the Marines were firmly in Iraq, another wife was having serious medical difficulties with her pregnancy. The CO allowed her husband to come home early to be with her as well. But it didn't even have to be a big thing, like a medical issue, for the XO to help out. When we had a new staff sergeant attach to the unit, his pay was messed up and it caused problems for his family; the command had it taken care of immediately.

It is fairly easy in the military community to paint the Marines as the bad guys—the ones who train too hard and don't care enough about the wives and children left at home. But Three-Four really tried hard not to lose sight of the families. Knowing that made military life and all the sacrifices it entails a little easier to deal with. Andy and the CO understood that.

The levity and the humor in his e-mails could turn a not-so-good day into a better day for me. And it helped knowing that I had someone there I could go to for advice and guidance. Andy never made me feel like the KVs were burdening him. He never even casually mentioned that we were creating extra work for him, which of course we were. The weird, wacky e-mails Andy and I sent back and forth helped keep me sane.

*January 18, 2004*
*Michelle,*
*Control freak? I am not, I just want things my way.*
*Very respectfully (sarcastically),*
*Andy*

*January 22, 2004*
*Andy,*
　*To quote a wise, spiritual leader . . . "I'm not a control freak,*
*I just want things done my way." (His Holiness the XO)*
　*Take care, oh wise and holy one (sarcasm? never heard of it)*
*Michelle*

Many months after the deployment had ended, Andy and I were laughing about everything that went on during the war, and he said that I had been his main contact with the "real world" throughout the deployment. I immediately apologized and said that if I had known that at the time, I would have been nicer to him!

All these e-mails stopped, though, once the battalion moved to Fallujah. It may have been security concerns, it may have been lack of access to computers and the Internet, I'm still not sure. But I do know that once the battalion entered the fight for Fallujah, I had to wait for Andy to call with information updates. And usually he would tell Paul something to pass on to me and then let Paul call me so we could have a few minutes over the phone. That is one thoughtful Marine—but don't tell him I said that.

# Chapter 17

# APRIL

April sucked. It's not a pretty sentence, but it works. April 2004 was a bad month. The battalion arrived in Fallujah at the beginning of the month, and it immediately made its presence known. Those of us back home still couldn't figure out why our guys had such a talent for getting right into the middle of everything. It was small comfort to know that they were good at their jobs, that the unit had a stellar reputation. We wanted them back somewhere safe watching the news coverage of Fallujah, not making the news.

I like to imagine the scene went something like this: General Jim Mattis looked out over all of the units in Iraq and said, "There's trouble in Fallujah. I need a unit to go down there and get dirty, get right in the midst of all the fighting and ugliness. You won't be able to shower, you won't have hot meals, you won't be able to call home. It won't be easy and not all of you will make it back."

There's stony silence in the room. Then from somewhere in the back a rumble starts, and General Mattis sees the Three-Four Marines raising their hands like second graders and standing on their tiptoes, "Oooh, oooh! Pick us, pick us!"

So off they go to Fallujah.

As for the KVs, our phone calls went from "How do I order more checks for my bank account?" (true call) to "Are there any casualties?" Suddenly we were right back in a war mentality. Tension and stress levels were back up. Phone calls and e-mails from our husbands stopped almost entirely. The news coverage was back to twenty-four hours a day on the standoff in Fallujah. Every day there were reports on IEDs and ambushes. I was watching Fox News nonstop again—except for brief intervals when Emily would watch *The Wiggles*.

We were getting only sporadic bits of information about the battalion. To get an idea of what was going on, all we could do was comb the newspapers and watch the news reports. Gunny Justice and the rear party were in contact with the battalion; they did their best to give us a picture of what was going on—and it wasn't a pretty picture. Our Marines were running operations into the city, hunting the bad guys, and capturing weapons. They were camped in and out of the city, participating in the psychological operations, running checkpoints, doing everything scary and dangerous that was being reported on the news. It was impossible for me to relax even a little bit knowing that Paul was so close to so much death and chaos.

Because Paul still had his satellite phone, he was able to call a few times during the Fallujah operations. Usually hearing his voice made me feel better, and I knew for a least those few moments that he was OK. There was one phone call though that only made things worse. We were able to talk for a few minutes when there was a huge boom in the background.

"What was that?" I asked.

"Oh, nothing," he said. "How's Emily?"

"She's fine. She's learning how to open the drawers in the kitchen, and she's climbing like a monkey." Then it happened again—*BOOM!* "Paul, what is that noise?"

"Uhh . . ."

"Is that gunfire?" Suddenly I have an involuntary mental image of Paul talking on the satellite phone while fighting goes on around him. Even though I knew that wasn't what was going on, I couldn't get the image out of my head.

"Mortars actually," he finally said.

"Ours or theirs?"

"Which would make you feel better?"

Not surprisingly he had to get off the phone pretty quickly after that. Paul had managed to sound so calm, but I carried the sound of those mortars echoing on the phone for a long time. I thought about sharing that story with some of the other wives, but I couldn't do it. Instead I kept it to myself and waited for another phone call.

Easter was coming up, so the KVs planned a get-together for the Three-Four wives and an Easter-egg hunt for the kids. We planned it for the Saturday before Easter at our favorite dinosaur park on base. The kids had a great time. Emily was a champion egg finder. Her basket was full, and I took plenty of pictures to send to Paul. As for the wives, most of us sat together discussing the coverage of Fallujah. Did anyone have any new information? Anyone get any phone calls?

Toward the end of the event, Gunny Justice got up to speak to the wives. He started talking about Fallujah and the dangers being faced there. Krista and I stared at each other. Was he really discussing casualties and notification procedures in front of the kids? I finally took Emily and walked away. Krista went over to Gunny and suggested that he wrap things up. It was an unfortunate downer for the day.

The next day was Easter, and Emily and I went down to Justine's house for another Easter-egg hunt. By now Emily had mastered the concept of finding eggs and putting them in the basket. We planned on having Easter dinner at Justine's house the previous night. It was another unofficial tradition. Justine and I had celebrated Easter together last year when both our husbands had been deployed to Iraq the first time. I decided to take Emily home for a quick nap before the dinner. I had just put her down in her crib when the phone rang.

"Hello?"

"Hey, honey, it's me."

*Paul!* "Hi. How are you? Happy Easter."

"Thanks. How's Emily?"

"She's fine. She loves Easter-egg hunts. We're having dinner with Justine tonight, and I just put her down for a nap. How are you? You sound tired." Actually he sounded awful.

"It's been a rough day. I need to tell you something, but you have to keep it to yourself for a while."

*Uh-oh. Never a good start.* "OK, what's wrong?"

"Oscar was killed." Lieutenant Oscar Jimenez was one of the unit's supply officers. He had been running resupply convoys back and forth from Fallujah.

"What?" My heart was pounding, my stomach twisting. "Oh my God. Poor Alli." *Oh God, Oscar was dead.* "What happened?"

"They were in a convoy, and they were ambushed. He was shot twice and killed."

Tears start to fall. Oscar and Alli were high-school sweethearts. They had three kids. And now he was just gone. No good-byes, no warning, just gone. "Thanks for telling me. We hadn't heard yet."

"You will. Alli's been notified, and the word will be coming from the rear party pretty soon."

"Are you OK?" I asked, tears rolling down my face. All I could think of was Alli and her kids.

"Yeah, I'll be fine. I . . ." Then he stopped. There wasn't much else to say. "I'll call you again soon. I love you. Kiss Emily for me."

"I will. I love you too."

I hung up the phone and just stood there in the kitchen. Just like that, a friend was gone and Alli was a widow. There was no preparation, just a phone call and it was done. Then the phone rang again.

"Hello?"

"Michelle? It's Krista."

"Hey, Krista. How are you?"

There's a pause. "Not too good. How are you?" She put a little extra meaning in the question.

So I answer carefully. "Not too good either. It's been a bad day."

"Yeah, me too. I just talked to Gunny Justice and I have some bad news."

*She knows.* "Paul just called me. I think he gave the same bad news."

"Oh God, Michelle, can you believe it?"

"No. What is Alli going to do?" Now we were both crying. "Krista, what should we do?"

"We need to call the KVs and let them know."

"And we need to call Alli's wives to make sure no one calls her when the rumors start about a KIA [killed in action] in the unit."

Then we both fell into silence. "I just can't believe it," I finally said. "She's one of us." It was a strange thing to say, but Krista knew what I meant. The battalion had had casualties before, but no one who had been married. No one we really knew, no one we hung out with or worked with had been affected yet. It was the first time one of our KVs had lost her husband. This was someone who lived right down the road, who had kids. This was real.

Right now Alli was hearing the news we all feared. Her husband was never coming home. I was sitting in my home, and I knew her life had changed the instant Gunny Justice had knocked on her door, but there was nothing I could do for her. As close as we all were, despite all the time we spent together, the laughter and sadness we had shared, this was the one thing none of us could help her with.

Gunny Justice had arrived at Alli's house in his dress blues and knocked on the door. Her house was full of family members who had driven up from San Diego to celebrate Easter with her. When Gunny began to tell Alli that Oscar had been killed, she ran upstairs and hid in the bathroom. She refused to listen to the news, as if closing her ears to it would make it go away. Oscar and Alli had been together for nearly fifteen years. Oscar had always taken care of her, now suddenly she was on her own.

The battalion lost three Marines that day. Oscar, Corporal Daniel Amaya, and Lance Corporal Torrey Grey. There were more Marines who had been injured in the ambush, and a few would be sent back to the United States for treatment. The impact of the ambush was devastating. Not only had one of our friends lost her husband, but the unit had also suffered a terrible loss. We were all feeling it—the new sense of dread and stress, the sick knowledge that people could be taken away that quickly. For those of us waiting and worrying, the stress became worse because there was nothing tangible we could fight, nothing solid for us to try to avoid or defend ourselves against. All we could do was wait and pray.

Krista and I split up the KV list, and we each called half. I told each one that Oscar had been killed and that Alli had been notified. Each call was met with shock and silence. Everyone wanted to know what they could do, but honestly we didn't know yet. I asked one of the other H&S Company volunteers to contact Alli's wives later that night and let them know that she would be their new KV. I asked her not to tell them about Oscar's death. It didn't seem right.

I didn't go to Easter dinner at Justine's, and she understood why. The next morning Justine volunteered to watch Emily while I went down to Alli's house. I made some banana bread and walked down the road to her house. I didn't even make it to the front door. Alli's family was already there in force. Her sister and brother were standing outside, and they wouldn't let me in to see her.

"How is she?" I asked. Stupid question.

"She's a mess," her sister said.

I explained who I was and gave them my phone number. I asked them to let Alli know that I had been by and to call if she needed anything. Then I gave them the banana bread.

"I know it's not much," I said, feeling utterly useless. "I just didn't know what else to do."

Her sister smiled at me, "It was very nice of you."

Then I went home. There were phone calls and questions, but none of it changed the fact that Oscar was dead and Alli was going through what we all feared the most. We all worried about her. She was always so quiet and reserved. We all knew that Oscar had done so much to take care of her and shelter her. It had been a big deal when she joined the KVN during the first deployment. How would she handle not only losing her husband, but also losing the whole life she had been leading for so many years? She would have to move, start over, and raise her children on her own. It was too much to think about, but Alli didn't have that luxury. This was her life now. And it broke my heart.

The following day Krista and Julie were able to get in to see Alli. Julie became one of Alli's biggest supporters. Cade and Oscar had worked together in the supply section of the battalion and were close friends, and I think Alli liked having Julie there. Julie was with her when Alli got the full report from the casualty officer of how Oscar had died. Julie was there when Alli had to go through the process of signing papers and dealing with the military life-insurance procedures. Julie was with her when Alli had to decide where Oscar's body should be sent and then make funeral arrangements. It could not have been easy on Julie, and I am so grateful that Alli had her to lean on during that time.

But Oscar, Daniel, and Torrey weren't the only deaths that month. Less than a week later we got word that the KV coordinator for Three-Seven lost her husband. Krista called and told me, and we were both just numb. I didn't know Sally very well, we had only met a few times at KVN events, but she and Krista were good friends. It was a shock. Not only because it was another friend, but because she was another "one of us." She shopped at the commissary with us, had children, and was active in the base community. She lived near Alli. And then all of the sudden, she was a widow. And to have both deaths happen so close together, it was overwhelming.

When Sally was notified of Rick's death, she opened the door and saw the Marines standing there. She asked them to wait outside while she sent her kids off to a neighbor's house. As the kids ran out the backyard gate to go play, Sally was letting in the Marines who would change her life forever. Her husband had been killed at the same time as another Marine who was married to a KV in Three-Seven. How many more would there be?

Fear and stress overtook all of us. Losing our husbands wasn't a far-off possibility anymore. It was real and close to home and any one of us could be next.

Krista and I called each other at least once a day. There was just so much going on with the wives, with our Key Volunteers, and with the battalion in Fallujah. And I think it helped both of us to have each other to call, vent to, cry with, or just compare notes on the day. One phone conversation just after we heard about Rick's death turned out to be more than either of us could handle.

"My plan is to ask for donations for flowers for Oscar's funeral at the next KV meeting." I explained. Krista was getting ready to have her baby, and she wouldn't be at the meeting.

"That's a good idea. Maybe we can also work out a schedule to bring over dinners for her and the kids so she won't have to cook."

"I'll bring it up." Then my doorbell rang. Krista must have heard it through the phone because she gasped.

"Was that your doorbell?" she asked quietly.

"Yeah." My heart was thumping. "Krista, don't hang up."

"OK. I'm right here."

"Have you heard anything?" I asked her as I walked to the door, and she knew exactly what I meant.

"No."

"OK. It's probably nothing." But there it was again—the fear, the nervous stomach, the slamming heart, the sudden vision of Gunny Justice in his dress blues waiting for me. And I opened the door to one of my neighbors, who just stopped by to drop off a package that had gone to her house by mistake.

"Are you OK, Michelle?" Krista asked when I told her what had happened.

"I'm fine. Just shaky. It's just that after Alli and Sally, it's starting to feel like bad luck to be a KV."

"God, Michelle, don't say that." We hung up right after all that, and later on we both admitted to having a good cry.

There was a bright spot in the midst of all this sadness. Krista's second son, Dylan, was born on April 20, 2004. Krista ended up having a cesarean section, and she had to go through it alone. I went to visit Krista the day after Dylan was born and brought her a bag of goodies; hospital food is bad everywhere and the Navy hospital was no exception. She looked good, and Dylan was beautiful. Krista's mother had come out to help take care of her older son, Kyle, while she was in the hospital. Her husband, Russell, had heard about the birth only a few hours afterward and had even been able to call the hospital and hear Dylan cry. The story goes that when word of Dylan's birth reached the battalion, they broadcast it over the radio so everyone could hear. Krista was even able to e-mail pictures of Dylan to Andy, who made sure that Russell got them. It wasn't the same as him being there—not even close—but they did get to share it as much as possible, and Krista solidified her position in my mind as the strongest woman I've ever met.

The day I visited Krista at the hospital, we talked about Oscar's funeral. It was the following day in San Diego. I had tried to organize a group of KVs to go down there, but as the day drew closer, people started dropping out. As I sat in Krista's hospital room, I was trying to come up with a decent excuse myself. Krista was very understanding and told me I didn't have to go. Then she managed to sneak in all the reasons why I should go. And she was right. Alli was my friend and one of my KVs, and she needed support. Oscar was my friend, and he died serving his country.

In the end there were four of us who went to the funeral: Stephanie Dillbeck, Lynde Phillips, Aime Fountain, and myself. My mom came out to watch Emily for me so I could go. I left early that morning and got to the church just before the funeral Mass started. I had parked a few blocks away, and when I got to the church I saw a big group of Marines in their dress blues standing in formation outside the church. I stood just behind them. It seemed natural for me to be with the Marines. Major Baker was there, and he saw me. He came over, gave me a hug, and said it was nice of me to have come.

A limo pulled up in front of the church. Alli and her kids got out of it and went straight inside. Alli was dressed all in black with dark sunglasses on, and she was carrying their youngest son. Just behind the limo, the hearse arrived and the Marines snapped to attention. My hands started shaking when they opened the back and gently lifted out the flag-draped coffin. *It's not Paul, it's not Paul*, I thought over and over and then felt horrible because it was Oscar. He was a good man, a loving husband, and a father who had died doing his duty.

When we filed into the ancient church, I found Stephanie, Lynde, and Aime, and we all sat together in the small wooden pews. Major Baker gave a moving eulogy and another of Oscar's friends gave a second one. The front of the church was decorated with flowers. Alli had requested red roses because they were special to her and Oscar, and I found the bouquet I had sent on behalf of the KVs. I also saw the red, white, and blue wreath from Julie Walton and another large arrangement Kerry McCoy had sent from her and Lieutenant Colonel McCoy.

Because it was a funeral Mass, communion was offered. I asked Stephanie in a whisper if she would be taking communion. It felt a little strange to me, but Stephanie went so I did too. When I walked past the altar, I glanced at Alli. She was staring off into space and still had her dark glasses on. Her youngest son was curled in her lap, and her two older children were crying.

From the church we drove in procession to the cemetery. The four of us from Twentynine Palms stood together under a tree as the graveside service was performed. Major Baker presented Alli with Oscar's Purple Heart. Taps was played, and I couldn't stop my tears. As the twenty-one-gun salute echoed in the quiet afternoon, the Marines beside the casket folded the flag that had draped Oscar's coffin throughout his journey home from Iraq. As Alli was presented with the flag, she started to rock back and forth, her lips pressed tightly together as she tried to stay strong for just a little bit longer. Then they lowered the casket into the ground, and we all sobbed. Oscar's mother fell on the ground beside the open grave and had to be carried away. Alli sat in her place the entire time and just stared at the lowering casket.

When the service ended, Major Baker came over to speak to us. Then we were joined by a young man with his arm in a sling. He was a young Marine who had been in the convoy with Oscar during the ambush. He had been wounded and sent back to Balboa Hospital in San Diego. His arm had been badly damaged, and he was probably going to be medically discharged from the Corps. But he had come to the funeral to offer his respect to both Oscar and Alli. He wanted to talk to Alli, but he didn't know if she would want to speak to him. He asked if we thought it was the right thing for him to do. We gave him our blessing. We watched as he went over to Alli and knelt on the ground in front of her. They spoke for a long while, and they both cried.

As the mourners began to leave, Stephanie, Lynde, Aime, and I walked over to talk to Alli. I gave her a hug and told her how sorry I was. To this day I don't know if she even knew I was there.

I decided not to go to the reception following the funeral. I just wanted to go home. I wanted to hold my daughter and look at pictures of my husband. I wanted to look at his clothes in the closet and sleep in our bed, and I wanted him to call. I needed him to call.

Paul did call that night, and I cried as I told him all about the service. He said the command wanted to know about it and how it went, so I said I would send an e-mail with the details to the XO. They had held their own memorial for Oscar, Daniel, and Torrey over in Iraq, as they did for any Marine killed, but Oscar was the first married Marine killed. I think they wanted to know that Alli was being taken care of and that Oscar received the same honors back home.

I also had to call Krista and Julie and give them the details because neither of them could make it to the funeral. That night I went to bed and prayed that I would never have to go through this again.

After Oscar's death, morale among the wives was low. Everyone was tense, and it was a sad time for all of us. I hosted a potluck dinner at my house about a week after Oscar's funeral for everyone who knew Alli. It was just meant to be a time for us to get together and talk, mourn, and draw strength from each other. Everyone showed up—including some friends who had left the battalion, but who had known Oscar and Alli. Alli didn't come, but that was OK, we all understood. At just this time a new KV, Rebecca Reyes, joined the group, and she had taken over calling Alli's wives. I felt bad that Rebecca joined us at such a sad time, but she was a blessing and jumped right in.

My house was in total chaos during the dinner. Kids of all ages were running around, more food than we could ever eat was piled high on the table, and there was an equal mix of laughter and tears. At one point, someone on the way out of my guest bathroom had closed the door, locking it from the inside. We had three pregnant women in the house, so that was not a good thing. Fortunately one of the other women there (a mother of two boys) knew how to use a bobby pin to jimmy the lock open. I was skeptical, but it actually worked. And the pregnant women rejoiced!

Andy even called my home phone during the event so he could be available to talk to the KVs. That was unexpected, but I took the phone on a tour of my house and let everyone who wanted to talk to him have a chance. I'm sure he was a little overwhelmed by it all, but he was a good sport. He hadn't seen my e-mail yet about the funeral so I found a quiet spot, gave him all the details, and made sure he knew that Alli was being taken care of. None of us knew if Alli would still be on base when the battalion returned home. She had six months to stay in her house on base, but we weren't sure if she'd want to. Fortunately, Julie was in frequent contact with Alli and was helping her through. Julie would let us know if there was something Alli needed, and then we'd do our best to organize it.

We were a tight community. Not just because our husbands were going through war together, though that certainly cemented the bonds, but also because of the very fact that we were military wives. Most of us were far from family and friends, we were living out in the middle of nowhere, and we knew we'd all be moving again shortly. Military wives have to make friends fast, and we all did. When Jennifer's daughter was born the previous year, we had organized a schedule to bring her and Tony dinner every night so they wouldn't have to cook. We did the same thing for Krista when Dylan was born. We all wanted to pull together for Alli, we just needed some guidance on how to do it. But Alli, being a very private woman, mostly wanted privacy and just a few close friends to talk to.

## Chapter 18

# THE LIGHT
# AT THE END
# OF THE TUNNEL

Paul spent our fourth wedding anniversary outside of Fallujah. He didn't send flowers to me this year, but he was able to manage a phone call, which was even better. For my birthday two weeks later (May can be an expensive month for my poor husband), he cleaned out my wish list at Amazon.com. I'm a fairly easy woman to shop for—books and jewelry, so that was a great gift. Julie and I had decided that when the battalion came home and started awarding medals to the Marines, we were going to put in for our own awards. We were going to call it the "deployment medal," and it should be awarded to all the wives who didn't divorce or cheat on their husbands. Of course we were looking at pretty, sparkly things for our medals—diamonds, sapphires— things that shine. I teased Paul about it, but Julie went so far as to send Cade pictures from her Tiffany & Co. catalog. Might as well put that combat pay to work!

Actually, the best anniversary present I got was an e-mail from the XO on May 13, 2004, saying that the battalion had left Fallujah and was going back to Haditha. We all breathed a big sigh of relief knowing that the Marines had moved back somewhere a little bit safer. They were still conducting operations, though, and we still had casualties. Marines would be sent out in small groups to go "find bad guys, capture bad guys." It continued to be dangerous work, and we all knew it. But just knowing they had made it out of Fallujah was a big weight off all our minds.

Once they were back at Haditha, the phone calls from our husbands started back up again. That was wonderful—

until the gossip started again. In one day I might get a phone call from a wife saying the Marines were coming home in June (which I knew wasn't true) and then another call from a wife saying the battalion was being extended through November (which I hoped wasn't true). It was frustrating, but we KVs did our best to address the issues. My standard response: wait until we hear something official from someone wearing green cammies.

In the end, the official word came from our favorite answer guy. Andy sent all the KVs an e-mail in May giving us the battalion's flight window. They were scheduled to come home between July 12 and July 16. Of course the flight window is a broad range of days that really only means that those are the days the battalion is scheduled to leave Iraq. There's no telling how long it will take them to get from Iraq to Twentynine Palms. But at least it was the information we had all been waiting for. Our Marines were scheduled to come home! But that was two months away. A lot could happen in two months—and it did.

With the light at the end of the tunnel, the wives became anxious again. First we went back to a bunch of the "silly calls"—wives calling about trivial matters. And somehow there was still genuine confusion over what the Key Volunteers actually do.

"Would you watch my children when my husband comes home?" *Uhhh . . . no.*

"Will you come clean my house before he gets home?" *Yeah, right.*

"Can I borrow your car?" *Ha!*

All I kept thinking was that we just had to make it to July 18. Then everyone would be home, no one would be upset anymore, and we'd all live happily ever after.

I think we all had short-timers syndrome. With so many of the Marines in the battalion getting ready to leave Three-Four once the deployment ended—either being transferred or getting out of the Marine Corps all together—everyone was just ready to move on. Even me. Paul was going to be leaving Three-Four in the fall of 2004 and transferring to the 7th Marine Regiment. That regiment was also based out of Twentynine Palms, so we wouldn't be moving. It was also halfway through a four-teen-month deployment to Iraq. One of the first things I asked him was if he would have to go back to Iraq with the regiment. The plan was for Paul to be part of the rear party, so he'd be staying on base—as long as they didn't need him in Iraq. I decided I was not going to think about that at the moment; one war at a time, please.

All that excitement and anxiety over getting ready and preparing to move didn't change the fact that we still had to get through this deployment. Sometimes it was hard to remember that when we all just wanted to get it over with and move on. I got to be a part of the reunion briefs this time around. I didn't do much—just stood up, gave my speech, answered some questions, and then let MCCS take over. There were already questions circulating about the next Three-Four deployment in January, and I felt so bad about that. Here I was, planning on getting my husband out of the unit, and I had friends who would be going through it a third time. There weren't many wives who would be facing a third Iraq deployment, but they were there. Kristy Hayes was one of them.

With only a few weeks left to go, more rumors started circulating. Marines were calling back home and telling their wives there was a possibility that the unit would suddenly be sent back to Fallujah. Talk about an uproar. The concern was that with the official transfer of authority in Iraq set to occur on June 30 might cause the insurgents to step up their activities, which would mean Three-Four would be needed back in Fallujah. We had some vengeful wives when that rumor began to fly. We were so close to the end of the deployment, they had flights booked, transfers were being lined up, and the advance-party Marines had already returned home. Was it possible they would take our guys and send them back to Fallujah? Quite honestly, with everything else that had happened during this second deployment, none of us would have been surprised. Mad, furious, hysterical, but not surprised. So, as usual, I went straight to my answer guy.

*June 26, 2004*

*Andy,*

*I've got a couple of upset wives who have been told (by their husbands) that they may be going back to that nasty town you visited a few months ago. This is not news I want to give to wives so can you please tell me this is not the case? And if, as I hope, no one is going back there, can you then please publicly flog any Marine who tells his wife such a thing.*

*Take care,*

*Michelle*

Andy replied to the rumor in an e-mail to all the KVs thus saving me a string of phone calls. (I told you he was thoughtful.)

*June 27, 2004*
*Ladies,*

*There is always the possibility that we might go back to the Fallujah area and operate. It is a contingency that we are preparing for as a precautionary measure. We have not been told we are going back. Please pass that to anyone that calls that we are only making plans so we can be ready.*

*We're almost to the finish line. Keep hanging in there, you are all doing a great job. Expect a lot of anxious phone calls the next couple of weeks and do your best to keep your sense of humor. I will pass schedules, flight information, etc as I get them. Let me know what rumor control I need to help squash.*

*Looking forward to seeing everyone soon,*
*Andy ———-*

Right as the Fallujah rumors were flying, Emily had her second birthday. Just like I had managed to prevent her from taking her first steps until Paul came home from the first deployment, I once again decided to fight nature, and I postponed her birthday. I figured she was only two (or now, one and thirteen months) and that she wouldn't mind too much if we just waited until her daddy came home to celebrate. Of course if the battalion had in fact been sent back to Fallujah and the deployment extended,

I would have thrown that idea out the window and let her have her birthday. But it was looking pretty good for the battalion to stay out of trouble and get home in July.

I had one other reason for not wanting the battalion to be extended. I was finally planning a honeymoon for Paul and me. When we got married, we were dirt poor and we didn't take a honeymoon. So after a baby and two deployments I figured we were due. Over numerous satellite phone calls we decided on a Hawaiian cruise. We were planning to go in September, and hoping that Paul would be out of Three-Four by then and wouldn't have any trouble getting leave. We still didn't have official block leave dates for the battalion yet, but I wanted to get the tickets booked (it's cheaper when you book in advance, you know). So I did. And when I mentioned it to Julie, she thought it was a great idea as well; she also booked a trip to Hawaii for her and Cade. Paul swore he could get the time off and that it wouldn't be a problem. But apparently Paul had forgotten to run it by the XO.

*June 21, 2004*
*Michelle:*
*What's this I hear about a cruise in September? What's next? Probably anarchy in the ranks. I just hope the new CO and XO are nicer than Lt. Col. McCoy and I am. I would deny the request and then hang pictures of Hawaii in my office so every time Paul and Cade came in to see me they would see it.*

*I suppose you and Julie will be trying to meet us at the airport or the armory as well. That way you can completely ignore*

*all the word we are passing. That's it, I quit. Delete my address
from the distribution list, it's every man for himself getting home.
If anyone needs me, I'll be smoking cigars on the back deck.*
   *Andy*

*June 21, 2004*
*Andy,*
   *Wow, the guilt . . . you must be Catholic. I haven't had a
guilt trip like that since Sr. Margaret chastised me for not having
Emily baptized as soon as she was born. Besides you know my
only purpose in life is to complicate your life . . . it gives me joy.*
   *Actually, Paul was supposed (I know you love that word) to
clear those dates with you over a month ago before we booked it.*
   *So, while you're on the back deck enjoying your cigar, let me
know if there is a problem with Paul getting leave in September.
I honestly thought he'd be out of 3/4 by that time. I don't really
want to make your life difficult . . . just challenging. Besides isn't
there a saying about absolute power corrupting absolutely?*
   *Take care (and stop sulking),*
   *Michelle*

In the end, Andy approved the requests, and both Paul
and I and Cade and Julie got our honeymoons.

As the battalion was getting ready to come home, all
the wives were getting jumpy and excited and desperate
for specific information on when their husbands would
arrive. The KVs were getting calls nonstop from the end
of June through the very day the Marines returned.

"When will my husband be home?"

"Which flight is he on?"

"When will the bus get to the base?"

It was all information that had to be coordinated between Twentynine Palms and Iraq, and even then it was still up in the air depending on how the airlines were doing. This was probably the most frustrating time of the deployment. They were so close to being home, but no one knew anything for certain. Wives were getting cranky, KVs were getting tense, and I was feeling those same emotions. I wanted to know exactly when Paul would be home. I wanted to know for certain that he was out of danger and that this chapter of our lives was over. The waiting was difficult for all of us.

I had given the KVs a standard line to tell any wives who called them wanting information: once we received the flight manifests that listed each flight and spelled out which Marine would be on which flight, the KVs would contact the wives and let them know when their husband was scheduled to come home. But until they received that phone call, we still did not have any information.

I wanted to prepare Emily as best as I could for Paul's homecoming. I kept showing her his picture and talking about Daddy coming home. She was older by now, and I think she understood the general concept of Daddy and that he would be back in the house, but the timeline was way beyond her. My biggest fear was that she wouldn't remember him and that she would cry as she had done at the reunion after the first deployment. I really didn't want Paul to have to go through that again.

It was July 5 before we got the first round of flight manifests. We at least now had an idea of which flights our husbands *should* be on. Of course anything could change right up to the time the planes actually left the ground. Paul was scheduled to be on the last plane out. This time I didn't even care—first flight, last flight, just get him home. I was counting down the days on the calendar and already planning for the next phase of our life. I didn't lose sight of the fact that they were still in a combat zone and still in danger, but it felt like we were really almost there. Just a few more days, and we will have made it.

In the midst of all this chaos, we were also trying to plan for the changes that would be coming once the battalion returned. Lieutenant Colonel McCoy was leaving, and Lieutenant Colonel Kennedy was taking over. Krista and Russell were transferring to Quantico within three weeks after he came back. Monica and Gene Coughlin were transferring to Okinawa as soon as he got back. Jennifer and Tony and Frank and Stephanie were all transferring to Camp Lejeune within a few months. Cade and Julie were leaving the Marine Corps and going back home to Texas. Paul was transferring out of the battalion to the 7th Marine Regiment. Andy was leaving Twentynine Palms to be General Mattis' aide. We were going to be losing over half of the Key Volunteers. And the battalion was scheduled to deploy once again back to Iraq only seven months after it returned. So while I was pestering Andy for the flight manifest and arrival times, he was after me to find the new Key Volunteer coordinator and to make plans to recruit new KVs. So don't feel too badly for the XO—he got to do his fair share of nagging too.

Fortunately for me, Krista was back in full force after her maternity leave (not that she actually got time off), and she took over the planning for the Key Volunteer Appreciation Dinner. With everyone planning on scattering once the Marines returned, we had to do this dinner as quickly as possible. So we (and by *we* I really mean Krista) planned it for the week after the Marines returned. This dinner is a traditional way for the command to say thank you to the Key Volunteers for their hard work. It's also a chance to say good-bye to all the women who were going to be leaving the unit. While I concentrated on getting the reunions and flights organized, Krista did all the work on dinner, gifts, and alcohol (lots of alcohol) for the KV event. I still don't know which of us got the worst end of that deal. But, hey we were both leaving the battalion within a month, so we didn't care about anything much past July anyway!

# Chapter 19

# REUNION

By the end of the first week of July, we were all planning for the reunion. Parents were flying in from all
over the country to be there when their sons returned.
Wives who had left the base to stay with family or friends
were returning and moving back into their base houses.
Phone calls were coming in constantly. I had people
calling asking for local hotel information, rental cars, and
airline information. Wives wanted to know when their
husbands could go on leave, when they could plan vacations, when transfer orders would come down so that they
could (in the words of one wife) "get the hell out of
Twentynine Palms."

But just when we thought we were out of the woods,
fate had one more curve ball for our Marines. About a
week before the flight window began, a fire ravaged
Three-Four's camp. By this time, the Marines were set up
in a tent city again, waiting for their flights to Kuwait. The
tents are doused in kerosene to keep the bugs away. Well,
some Marine (from a different unit) had been smoking
next to one of those kerosene-covered tents and tossed his
cigarette away. *Poof!* Fire in tent city.

None of our Marines were hurt, and the fire was put
out quickly, but a lot of Marines lost everything—
uniforms, personal items, military gear. Paul had packed up
most of his belongings by this time. All the stuff he had
stored in boxes and ready for the flight home, including all
of his Starbucks coffee, went up in smoke. His Marines
helpfully told him that "at least the smoke smelled good,
sir." But he also lost all the letters I had written him and

pictures of Emily. It was a shock, and none of us could really believe it.

We had to make another round of phone calls to the wives of the battalion and let them know what had happened. Most of them wanted to know what they could buy for their husbands so they would be stocked up when they got home. It made for a rush on uniforms and boots at the base uniform shop over the next few days.

There wasn't much we could do except laugh. This deployment had been so crazy, so full of ups and downs and stress—it just made sense that there would be a fire a week before our Marines left to go home. That's just the way this deployment had worked: Instead of going to Okinawa, they went back to Iraq. Then they went to Fallujah. Now there's a fire. What else could happen? None of us were going to believe that the worst was over until we finally had our husbands back in our arms. That became our only focus—just bring them home. I don't care how you do it. Just get them back home.

The Key Volunteers sponsored another sign-making party just before the flight window began. But I didn't make a sign for Paul this time around. I had talked to Alli, and she said seeing the welcome home signs hanging on the fence and all over the base broke her heart. She had decided to stay on base until she could find a home for her and the kids, and now she would be there when her husband's unit came home. As much as I wanted to welcome Paul home and I wanted him to know how much I loved him, I just couldn't make a sign this time around. Paul and I never talked about it, but I'm sure he noticed it. Krista didn't make a sign for Russell, either—not because of Alli, but because she had a nineteen-month-old and a newborn.

The last few weeks leading up to the battalion's home-coming were just as hectic as the first deployment—crash diets, frantic house cleaning, welcome-home gifts. Poor Julie Walton had the worst of it though.

Less than a month before the battalion returned, Julie finally got word that a house on base had opened up. She was thrilled and wanted desperately to have everything moved into the new house and set up before Cade came home. So she worked like a mad woman moving with their daughter into the base house. Then the day the moving company brought her stuff, crisis! The movers had taken her door off the hinges in order to get her furniture moved in. Then a fight broke out between the movers. There was yelling and cursing, and then the truck just took off, leaving Julie behind with her door still off the hinges and her furniture only partially moved in. Julie slept on the floor that night with her front door propped up against the frame. Fortunately the owner of the company felt appropriately rotten about it all and came by the next day to finish the moving and to fix her door. I don't know why any of us were surprised—that was just the way this deployment had gone. Bring it on, what else have you got?

Paul was again coming in on the last flight, as was Andy. Most of our friends, including Russell Boyce, Cade Walton, Tony Johnston, and Frank Dillbeck, came in on a flight a few days prior to Paul's. They didn't get back to the base until after midnight. But Krista, Julie, Jennifer, and Stephanie were all there—with kids in tow—to meet those buses. Russell finally got to meet his new son, and there were tears and hugs and kisses all through the night.

Paul and Andy were due to arrive on base around 1 p.m. on July 18. It was pushing 115 degrees that day, but Emily and I were there early, just in case. I had Emily all dressed up in a cute little blue dress with a matching hat that my mom had bought for her. I once again failed to dress up—it was just too hot! We ended up waiting for nearly two hours at Victory Field, a large grassy area used for base events. Having the reunions take place on the field rather than at the gym worked out nicely. Gunny Justice did a great job organizing the event, we had tents set up to provide some shade, and MCCS was there with water and snacks. We also had corpsmen walking the area looking for cases of possible sunstroke. One of them kept following Emily around because her cheeks were so red. (She was two, and she didn't get the whole concept of sitting in the shade and staying cool. She was off and running and checking everything out—and so of course I was running after her.)

Lieutenant Colonel McCoy had flown in earlier, and he was there with Kerry. It was wonderful to see both of them, and I got a big hug from the CO. I thanked him for keeping my husband safe, and he thanked me for keeping the wives sane. He was getting ready to pass command of Three-Four on to Lieutenant Colonel Kennedy and then transfer back to Quantico. It was nice that he and Kerry would finally be stationed in the same state!

The local radio station covered the progress of the buses from the air force base to Twentynine Palms. MCCS had the radio piped in through a loudspeaker, and every thirty minutes or so we'd get an update. The radio station did this every time a group of Marines came back to the base. And every time people would come out and line the road to wave, cheer, and welcome the Marines home. These weren't family members waiting for loved ones—these were people from the community who heard the Marines were returning and just wanted to show their support.

When we finally heard that the buses had reached the front gate, we all cheered and the radio station played Thin Lizzy's "The Boys Are Back in Town." It was a great moment and the crowd really started to buzz.

But we still had another hour to wait. The Marines had to go to the armory first to turn in their weapons and then get back on the buses for the final ride to Victory Field. While I was waiting and chasing Emily, someone tapped me on the shoulder.

I turned around, expecting it to be another wife or family member. "Andy!"

The XO was back, looking tired but safe. I gave him a hug and asked a million questions at once. The most prominent one being "Where's my husband?"

"They're still at the armory."

"How are you? No bullet holes? Do you have family here?" He was actually on his own, because he was planning to visit his family back home in Massachusetts a few weeks later. He was also the guy in charge of making sure all the Marines stayed out of trouble on their first night back. He must have been the only Marine in Three-Four not to get the day off. We talked for a bit and then I took him to some of the other Key Volunteers and reintroduced him.

Then at last, the roar started. The crowd rushed forward to the chain link fence separating the field from the road. People were yelling and waving and shouting; the buses were coming into view. Four large white buses slowly made their way down the road. I grabbed Emily, didn't even say good-bye to whomever it was that I was talking to and tried to find a visible place to stand. I opted for the far end of the fence where it was less crowded.

"Emily, Daddy's coming home."

"Daddy, Daddy!"

I was already crying when the doors to the buses opened and the first Marines stepped down. The crowd cheered. People were laughing and crying and screaming out names, holding up signs. Marines stepped off the buses and walked with all their gear toward the openings in the fence line. Then they would spot their wife/child/mother/father, and huge grins would appear their faces. All the fatigue and pain of the past seven months would disappear in that instant.

Paul wasn't the last one off the bus this time, and I knew him the second he stepped down.

"Paul! Paul! Over here!" He spotted us and smiled. He walked to the nearest break in the fence, and I made my way toward him with Emily. We met halfway, and when he took me in his arms I couldn't even see past the blur of tears running down my face. *He's home. He's safe. Thank you, God. It's finally over. We made it.*

"God, I love you," he said and held me like he wouldn't ever let me go.

"I love you too. I'm so glad you're home."

"Me too."

We found a small piece of shade under the tent, and he dropped all his gear. He took off his sunglasses and his cover and knelt down in front of Emily. I could see the trepidation in his eyes. But Emily only needed one look at him.

"Daddy!!" And she went right into his arms. I cried and then fortunately remembered to take pictures. Paul lifted her up and held her close.

"I missed you so much, little girl." He kissed her and squeezed her until she squirmed. When he put her down, he reached into his pack and pulled out a teddy bear. Emily grinned and grabbed it.

"It was bribery," Paul admitted sheepishly. "Just in case she didn't remember me again."

"But she did," I said.

"Yeah, she did." He couldn't stop grinning.

Unlike the first reunion, this time we actually spent some time down at the field talking with friends. Paul's Marines came up to us and asked to meet me or to introduce Paul to their wives, girlfriends, or parents. Moms and dads stopped Paul to thank him for taking care of their sons.

When we finally began to make our way back to the car, a reporter spotted us. He raced in front of us and started snapping pictures of Paul carrying Emily. Someone had given Emily an American flag to wave while we were waiting for the buses, and she was still holding it. It made for a great picture: Paul holding Emily in her cute dress waving an American flag. It showed up on the front page of the paper the next day.

By the time we got home, Emily was already used to Daddy being back, and she was jabbering away at him. Just like with the first deployment, I made Paul dump all his gear and uniforms in the garage until everything could be washed. I had steak, Guinness, and a pile of welcome-home gifts waiting for him. Emily helped him open all the gifts, and he just sat back and watched her, amazed by how much she had grown while he had been gone. His favorite gift was waiting in the backyard. I had bought him a new grill, and he was ecstatic. I even left it in the box for him so he could put it together. That was actually part of the gift too—manual labor.

I made a few phone calls that night to family just to let them know Paul was back and that he was still in one piece. All the calls were kept short and sweet. We knew we'd be bombarded with questions and visits within the next few weeks, so we took that first night just for us. Once Emily went to bed, Paul and I sat out in the family room (that I had redecorated again while he had been gone). Paul drank his beer and I sat curled against his side.

"I love you," I said.

He held me tight against his side. "I love you too. I missed you every day."

"Do you want to talk about it?" I saw even from that first day that Paul had seen too much, done too much, and had scars I couldn't see. There was a seriousness about him that hadn't been there before, a look in his eyes that I couldn't name or understand.

"No. Not right now."

"OK." And instead of talking about all that we had done, everything that had gone right and wrong, we just sat there together. And that was enough.

# Chapter 20

# HAIL AND FAREWELL

We had the Key Volunteer Appreciation Dinner only a week after the Marines returned. Krista had arranged to have it at the Officer's Club, and it was a wonderful night. All the KVs were there with their husbands, and it was the perfect opportunity to tell all the Marines how much work their wives had done. Paul and I sat with Krista and Russell, Lieutenant Colonel and Kerry McCoy, Andy, and Sergeant Major Howell. I think even my husband was impressed that he was sitting at the front table. Of course when we were doing the seating arrangements Paul begged me not to seat him next to the CO.

"What would we talk about?" he worried.

"Me," I offered. He was not impressed.

In the end, Russell Boyce sat next to the CO, I sat next to Krista, and Paul sat next to Andy. The rest of the KVs and their husbands were arranged by the company they were with. Lieutenant Colonel McCoy even made all the company commanders come to the dinner (in coat and tie, no less) and show their appreciation to the KVs. I didn't feel too badly for them though—the drinks were free.

Over dinner I found out that of the eight people at our table, five of them had already run the Marine Corps Marathon at least once. Only Paul, the sergeant major, and I hadn't done it. When Krista tried to talk me into running it one day, I gave her my standard marathon response: "If I ever need to go twenty-six miles, I'll drive."

After dinner, Krista and I handed out awards and gifts to the KVs. Lieutenant Colonel McCoy got to stand up there with us and pass out beautiful Christmas ornaments he and Kerry had purchased to show their appreciation. I made a point to say something nice about each and every KV. I wanted to make sure that their husbands had a chance to hear that their wives had made a difference during the deployment and that they deserved to have their efforts recognized. By the end of the presentations I was ready to cry. I presented Andy with a plaque we had ordered for him, but I couldn't think of a single thing to say. What could I say about the man who had made sure we had everything we needed to take care of our wives? He had been generous and kind and funny and had never once complained. A plaque would never be enough.

Then Krista and I had to say our good-byes to each other. We were both teary, and our husbands just shook their heads at us. The KVs had all chipped in to buy me a lovely silver plate that Krista had engraved. And we had all put together a scrapbook for Krista. It had been a comedy of errors before the dinner began, as Krista and I each ran around to all the KVs, trying to get them to sign cards for the other one without each other seeing. So Krista and I blubbered through our tributes to each other and then tried not to think of the fact that she was leaving in only two weeks. What would I do without her daily phone calls and e-mails? I introduced Kristy Hayes as the new Key Volunteer coordinator and then told everyone to start calling her. Everyone laughed, but just like that, my job had ended, and Kristy was in charge. Kristy would be leading the KVs through another Iraq deployment in only six months. Just as I was finally celebrating the fact that my husband was home for good, Kristy was preparing to go through it all again. I guess that is the way the Marine Corps has always worked—it never ends. There is always someone ready to take your place and pick up the fight.

By August 2004, people were leaving. Lieutenant Colonel McCoy passed command of Three-Four on to Lieutenant Colonel Kennedy and then transferred to Quantico. None of us knew what he and Kerry would do once they finally got to live in the same house. Krista, Russell, and their two boys sold their house and transferred to Quantico as well. In fact, Russell was working for Lieutenant Colonel McCoy again. Andy left to work as General Mattis' aide in Quantico. Jennifer, Tony, and their daughter transferred to Camp Lejuene and bought their first house. Frank and Stephanie followed soon after.

We had a going-away dinner at the Twentynine Palms Inn for Jennifer just before she left. When we were all standing in the parking lot after dinner, lingering over good-byes, Jennifer said something I will never forget. We were talking about moving to a new duty station and having to make new friends and getting to know everyone when she told me how the two Iraq deployments had changed her perspective on friendship.

"It's not going to be so easy for me to make new friends now," she said.

"Why?"

"Because having gone through this war with all of you, I know what real friendship means. Now whenever I meet someone new I'll have to ask myself, 'Could I go to war with you?'"

And I understood exactly what she meant. All the other stuff that goes on in military life—the coffees, the social events, the gossip, the moves—none of that matters when you're suddenly faced with your husband going to war. When that happens, you want to have people you can count on. Those are the friendships that last, and that's why it hurt so much to see all of them leaving.

Paul and I weren't going anywhere. Paul transferred to 7th Marine Regiment and became part of its rear party. The regiment was seven months into a fourteen-month deployment when Paul transferred in. My fear was, of course, that he was going to be sent back to Iraq. Paul said he would only have to go if something happened to the communications officer who was already over there. Gee, I wonder why that didn't make me feel any better?

Not long after we moved to the regiment, I bumped into Colonel Tucker's wife Elizabeth at a family event, and she grabbed me as soon as she saw me.

"Are you at regiment now?"

"Yes, Paul is the rear party communications officer."

"Do you want to be our KV coordinator?"

*Uhh, didn't I just do this?* "Well," I began cautiously. "I would be very glad to help out. But with me just transfer-ring in and Paul not deploying, maybe I'm not the right person to be the coordinator."

"No," Elizabeth insisted. "You'll be perfect. We're in a bit of a bind." She went on to tell me that their previous

KV coordinator had been relieved (a fancy military word for fired). So now they needed someone new to step into the role.

As Elizabeth stood in front of me, waiting for my reply, I had a sudden insight into my personality. I am apparently incapable of saying no to anyone. So instead of politely declining and explaining that after two deployments I could really use a break, I heard the distant echo of my own stupid voice saying, "Sure, Elizabeth. I'd love to do it."

Paul laughed hysterically when I told him what had happened. He laughed even harder when we found out that the regiment was getting a new family readiness officer—Gunny Justice, who was also transferring to the regiment. But I don't think anyone told him that I had volunteered to take over as the KV coordinator. At the first meeting I ran as the coordinator, Gunny Justice walked in, and when he saw me, he froze. I could almost hear the curse words forming in his brain. And the first item on my agenda? The newsletter. And so it started all over again. At least this time I had Paul to talk to every night. But I felt rotten every time I ran a meeting or organized a family event, because my husband was home. I was giving information to the families, answering their calls, but I got to see my husband every day. I felt guilty, I felt bad, but I wouldn't have wanted him to deploy again for anything, which made me feel even guiltier.

In September, just after Paul's transfer, we were able to take our long-delayed honeymoon. We left the day before Paul's birthday. My dad and stepmother had volunteered to watch Emily for us for the two weeks we'd be gone. Our cruise left from Vancouver and ended in Honolulu. I love Hawaii, and Paul had never been there before. It was the perfect vacation for us. We were lazy and happy and together.

The cruise had two formal nights, and I had insisted that Paul bring his dress blue uniform for them. He was quite the sight walking around the ship. The first formal night we walked into the dining room, and everyone stared—and not at me, which would have been bad for my ego if I hadn't been so proud. As soon as we were seated, a bottle of wine appeared at our table, complements of another passenger. For the rest of the night, people stopped us. Men and women came up to shake Paul's hand and thank him for his service. They wanted to know if he had been to Iraq, and when he said yes, they all wanted to buy him a drink or shake his hand again. Former Marines were telling Paul stories from Vietnam, Korea, even World War II. Paul and I had been taking ballroom dance lessons aboard the ship, and when we tried out our waltz that night an older man and his wife stopped us in the middle of the floor. The man had been a Marine over fifty years ago. Since the time he had gotten out of the Corps, he had had a career, retired, and traveled the world, but he still remembered his Marine Corps days like they were yesterday. He had only been in for three years, but he still considered himself a Marine.

"Once a Marine, always a Marine, right?" He grinned and slapped Paul on the back. His wife stood by my side and just smiled, like she had heard these stories a thousand times. Then she looked at me and took my hand.

"And thank you for your service," she said.

As she held my hand, I didn't know what to say. That entire night when people stopped to talk to Paul, they didn't pay much attention to me. A few would look at me and say, "Oh, you must be so proud."

"Yes, I am," I would reply. "I'm happy that he's home."

But here was this woman, holding my hand, and she knew. She got it. She remembered the worry, the pain, the fear from all those years ago when her husband had gone to war. It was fifty years ago, but she still remembered. And I knew then that no matter how many years went by, no matter what else Paul and I would go through in our life together, the war would always be there. I knew I would never forget.

"Thank you, ma'am," was all I could say.

For the rest of the cruise, Paul was getting free drinks. We almost always had company for breakfast. He wore his uniform again for the second formal night, and the same thing happened. People wanted to be near him, to share a story, or to offer their thanks. He even got a number of looks from the single women on the ship. Fortunately for him, and them, I am not a jealous woman.

We were able to enjoy our two weeks in paradise, and it was the perfect time to get to know each other again. We hiked in a bamboo forest in Maui, went kayaking in Kauai, waited for the sunrise on Haleakala, shopped in Old Town Kona. Then we went back to the ship and danced and ate and watched the shows. Neither of us wanted it to end. But eventually we had to return home to Twentynine Palms.

By the time we got back, Three-Four was in full training for the deployment to Iraq. Every once in a while Kristy Hayes would call me for advice. Paul had trained his replacement to take over the Three-Four communications platoon, but as the date of the deployment drew closer, I could see Paul was torn. He didn't want to leave us again, he didn't want to miss any more of Emily's life, but having to stand by and watch some of his Marines prepare to go back to combat without him was hard on him. He knew he had done his job and that it was time to turn it over to someone else, but I could see him watching the Marines with a strange mix of envy and worry.

That November, Paul was promoted to captain. The ceremony took place outside of Three-Four's headquarters. I pinned on one of Paul's captain's bars, and Major Matt Baker did the other one. My mom came out for the ceremony, and she stood off to the side, holding Emily's hand. Then from out of nowhere Emily shouted "Captain Daddy!" and everyone laughed.

Not long after his promotion, Paul and I went to Three-Four's Marine Corps Birthday Ball. Because the regiment was deployed, they weren't having a ball that year, so Paul and I and a few other former Three-Four Marines went to the Three-Four ball instead. The ball actually made it all the way into Las Vegas that year. No more little hotel just on the Nevada side of the state line—

instead it was big hotels, casinos, and mirrors on the ceilings of every room (that's the truth). The ball was fun, and well organized, but it just wasn't the same. There were new faces, new people, and so many of our friends had already moved on. Paul and I and Cade and Julie ended up sitting with Sergeant Major Howell because no one had given us table assignments. That was actually a lot of fun because the sergeant major had just gotten married and was trying to keep it quiet. Well, that didn't last too long with Julie and me at the table with his new wife.

But by the time the dinner and ceremony parts of the evening ended, Paul and I and Cade and Julie ended up at the bar. Frank and Stephanie Dillbeck joined us there. We were all feeling a little out of place. We weren't part of the new command, we didn't know the majority of the people there, and we were all too busy looking at the new CO and XO and thinking how much we missed Lieutenant Colonel McCoy and Andy. So the six of us spent the night drinking and reminiscing and drinking some more. There even was a Vegas lounge act in the bar, so we were happy as could be.

I think the guys had concocted a conspiracy to get their wives drunk, because Julie, Stephanie, and I were the ones at the bar most of the time. We took turns ordering different shots for the three of us. Julie ordered caramel apple shots for us, and we downed them as our husbands cheered us on in their dress blues. Then Stephanie waltzed up and ordered three shots of whiskey. Julie and I just stared at her for a second, but we joined her and won the eternal respect of our Marines. I got the next round; I can't remember what is was, but we drank it. Then we danced and laughed and toasted all of our friends who couldn't be there. One for Krista. One for Jennifer. One for Alli. One for Lynde, Jessica, Monica, Aime, and everyone else we missed. The good news: our husbands made sure we all made it upstairs safely.

# Chapter 21

# MOVING ON

Not long after the Marine Corps ball, Paul and I found ourselves left alone on base. Frank and Stephanie and their two children had transferred to Camp Lejuene. Cade and Julie and their daughter had left the Marine Corps and moved back to Texas. I was now the experienced wife on base. I had been there for over two years, and I knew all the answers. I'd take Emily for a walk down to the park, and other moms would ask me questions about the base, where to shop, and how far away Disneyland was.

By now, Three-Four had gone back to Iraq, this time without my husband. I wanted to feel bad about that, but I was just so thankful that he was home. We went together when the buses left and waved good-bye to the Marines, knowing that we would already have transferred to another duty station by the time they returned. Nothing in the Marine Corps stands still for very long.

In March 2005, Paul finally got his transfer orders. We had spent nearly two months trying to figure out where we were going to go next. Every time Paul asked for my input I gave him the same response, "I just want you to be home for a while." I didn't care too much about where we went, I only wanted him out of the deployment cycle. I wanted to have my husband come home every night, and I wanted him to be with Emily.

After much debate, Paul ended up getting a desk job in Quantico. He would be doing computer-network security for the Marine Corps. And while the job description involved a lot of technical words that I didn't understand,

Paul was really excited about it. In May, all of our furniture disappeared as the movers came and packed us up. Between everyone who had transferred and the new deployment, there weren't many people left on base for us to say good-bye to—it felt like we were the last ones to leave.

On Mother's Day, Emily and I drove up to my dad's house in Santa Rosa. Paul had to stay behind to make sure the house on base passed inspection before he could officially check out. Meanwhile, he was trying to arrange for a house on base in Quantico, but nothing was available. So we decided to be adventurous and buy our first house. We flew out to Quantico and had a whirlwind week looking at houses, applying for the mortgage, and going through all the paperwork.

Settling in to life back in Quantico was a lot like déjà vu. Krista and Russell Boyce were living just a few streets away from the house we bought, and Andy and Lieutenant Colonel McCoy were both working a few buildings away from Paul's new office. One of our first stops when we moved back to Virginia was Andy's new office. While we were there, General Mattis came out, and Paul and I were reintroduced to him. When Andy said that we had been with Three-Four, General Mattis broke into a big grin.

"Those boys could fight," he said and shook Paul's hand again.

Krista was the first visitor we had at our new house, and she even brought cookies. Not long after we moved in, she and Russell hosted a barbecue. When we got there, it was an unofficial Three-Four reunion. The Boyces, the

McCoys, Andy, the Fountains, Sergeant Major Howell and his wife, and a whole group of other Three-Four veterans. Lieutenant Colonel McCoy joked that we had become "Three-Four East." The CO (because I will always think of him as the CO) gave me a hug and welcomed us back to the East Coast.

"It's great to see you again," he said.

"Thank you, sir, you too."

"Michelle," he said, suddenly very serious. "How many times do I have to tell you to call me Bryan?"

I think he made me blush, then and there. "That's the last time . . . Bryan." But that just doesn't sound right, does it?

Later, I was able to sit down with Andy and catch up with him. He was working nonstop with General Mattis. They were traveling all over the world, and I teased him about the fact that even though he was out of Three-Four, he still didn't have a life.

That night I had made two desserts to bring to the barbecue. I made a fruit trifle for the guests and a special chocolate soufflé cake for Sergeant Major Howell. As it turns out, part of the reason for the big get-together was that the sergeant major was going back to Iraq. He had transferred to a reserve unit, which had been activated and was being sent to Iraq for a year. It was a reminder to all of us that while we were talking and laughing, we still had friends in Iraq. It may have been over for all of us, but it wasn't really over.

I think all of us knew that the deployments had been something special, a time and a group of people that couldn't be recaptured. There were bonds between all of us now that went beyond just serving together or being neighbors. Our husbands had gone through war together. The wives had gone through the worry and the waiting together. We could see it at that first barbecue. While the guys were grouped together over their beers and cigars, sharing stories of Baghdad, Haditha, and Fallujah, we wives were sharing our war stories. And as time went on, those stories started to seem strange and distant, like we were talking about a movie we had all seen. Did we really go through that? Was that really what our lives had been like? What had we been thinking? I think we each finally began to ask ourselves what the rest of the world had been asking us for months: How did we do that?

Of course nothing in the Marine Corps is ever easy, as all of us who left Three-Four looking for something less hectic soon found out. Paul's desk job—the one that didn't include deployment—did include frequent trips across the globe. He was gone an average of one to two weeks out of every month. And Russell Boyce was gone even more than Paul. Krista and I figured that with the amount of travel they were doing, we might average one husband between the two of us. There are days where I am bitter and resentful; after all, I have already lost more than a year with my husband. I just want him to be home at night for dinner like a normal family. But life in the Marines isn't normal. You'd think I'd have learned that by now.

And as if the new house (which we were remodeling ourselves, because we are, in fact, that dumb) and Paul's new job wasn't enough, we had one more surprise in store. Two days after Christmas, 2005, I found out that I was pregnant again. My exact reaction when the stick turned blue? "Oops."

Now I had sworn up and down that after going through two deployments with a baby that I wouldn't have another child as long as Paul was in the Marine Corps. As long as he was a Marine, there was always a chance that he would be sent off to another combat zone. I just couldn't imagine going through that again, but this time with two children. Besides, Emily was perfect and wonderful and what would I do with another baby anyway? My ally in this only-child plan was Julie Walton. She and I decided we would take pride in our one-child status. So when I found out I was going to be booted out of the only-child club, I dreaded having to tell her. I ended up chickening out of calling her, and I sent her an e-mail. It didn't take her long to call.

"Hey, Michelle. It's Julie."

*Gulp. Here it comes.* "Hi, Julie."

"So . . . how are you?"

"Well, I'm pregnant."

"Me too!"

*What?* "What did you say?"

"I'm pregnant too. Can you believe it?"

She and Cade were having their own surprise baby. The funny thing is that we even had the same due date, September 4—Labor Day, of course! We were talking and e-mailing constantly from that time on. I wished so badly that we were all back in Twentynine Palms so we could be going through it together, but life goes on.

Julie gave birth to a beautiful daughter on August 20, 2006. I followed her five days later when our son, Brett Matthew, was born. Paul was ecstatic to be a father again, and looked forward to watching his new son go through all the baby milestones he had missed with Emily.

Our time in Twentynine Palms had been full of ups and downs and then it was over. Now there was someone else going through the worry and the fear, someone else waiting for a knock on their door, someone else praying that it would never come. It somehow manages to hurt just a little knowing that life in Three-Four and in Twentynine Palms is going on just fine without us. We were there, we did our jobs, and then we left. If you mentioned my name to someone back at Twentynine Palms today, nine times out of ten they'd have no idea who I was—just like I didn't know the men and women who had come before me in Three-Four. But even though no one there remembers me or Paul or what we went through, we remember.

There will always be a group of men and women who know exactly what those months during the war were like. Krista, Jennifer, Julie, and all the others know, and they will always remember. It's not a coincidence that in all the years that Paul and I have been in the Marine Corps, and all the people that we have met, that the ones I still keep in touch with the most are the women from Three-Four. Krista and I see each other all the time. We get together for "Moms' Night Out" adventures, getting away from our husbands and our kids for a few hours and having some adult conversation. Krista has even taken it upon herself to organize reunions for the wives from Twentynine Palms. The reunions take place once a year, usually in March, and she has dubbed them the "Marine Wives Gone Wild" weekend. In 2006, wives came from all over the country to be together. That is how deep the bonds that were formed in the midst of the war have gone. I pray none of us will have to go through a deployment like that again, but I also know that with the right group of women, it's possible to endure anything.

# Chapter 22

# LESSONS LEARNED

The cliché says that when you hold your baby in your arms for the first time you forget the pain of child-birth. Personally, that didn't work for me—labor is still very clear in my mind—but at least I understand the senti-ment. Time and distance can change our perspective. Looking back on those two years of deployments and war, I remember the good days and the bad days, the night-mares and the fear, but with more detachment. When I mention that time in conversation, my stomach doesn't flip and my chest doesn't tighten. It's just another story, just another event in our lives. I think that's what worries me the most sometimes. What does it say about me that I can look back on my husband going to war and see it now as *normal?* Maybe I am crazy after all. Or maybe I'm just a Marine Corps wife. Maybe all of us are crazy.

It's been two years since Paul returned from his last Iraq deployment. We have moved, bought a house, and had our fights and make-ups along the way. The war is still with us, but it has moved to the background. We have two pictures on the wall from those deployments. The first is the photo of Paul holding the Iraqi girl from the first deployment, the second is the photo of Paul and Emily when he came home from the second deploy-ment. I see those pictures every day, but sometimes I just pass right by them and don't even notice that they're there. Then one of our friends will come over or we'll have a dinner party, and someone will notice the pictures and ask about the war. Then we'll talk and share our stories over wine. We'll remember that there are still men and women fighting and dying, and there are still families back home waiting for news. Our roles in the war are over, but the war itself goes on.

When Paul came back from the second deployment, he was a different man. He was still my husband, my best friend, and a wonderful father, but he had been changed by all that he had seen and done. He laughed less. He was more serious and quieter than he had ever been before. For a long time he didn't want to tell me about his experiences in Iraq. Every time I brought it up, he said he didn't want to talk about it yet. It took months and me asking specific questions to get him to open up about it at all.

"Did you ever have to draw your weapon?"

"Yes." And that was it.

So I'd wait a few more days or weeks until I had another opening in the conversation. Once we were driving and Paul was talking about the way they awarded different medals and the requirements for each one.

"Did anyone ever shoot at you?" I asked.

"Yes." And that was it.

"Did they ever come close?" I finally asked.

"Yes." And then he changed the subject.

Little by little I began to hear stories about what Paul had been through. He didn't sit me down and tell me everything, but he would tell someone else and then I would find out. When we went to San Diego to finally have Emily baptized at the church where we were married, we were able to visit with our good friend Sister

Margaret. She gave Paul a huge hug and then smacked him on the shoulder for making her worry about him. Of course Sister Margaret is a sixty-year-old Irish nun; we don't mess with her.

"I'd just about worn through my knees praying for you," she said in her lilting Irish brogue.

"Well, I'm grateful for it," Paul replied. "I know those prayers saved my life at least once." He then went on to tell her about a day in Fallujah when he had been driving in his Humvee. The battalion was under heavy fire, and a mortar round landed less than two feet from his front bumper. He had never told me that story. When I asked him why later that day, he just said, "I didn't want you to worry."

I know there's more he hasn't told me, more he will probably never tell me, but I understand. He's home now, and we've moved on. The memories are still there and always will be, but now they're just memories—memories and stories to share at barbecues.

William Jennings Bryan has a quote that I found not long after Paul left on the second deployment: "Destiny is not a matter of chance, it is a matter of choice." I tried to keep that thought in mind while Paul was gone. I never had a choice in Paul being sent to war, but I did have a choice in the way I dealt with that fact. I could spend all his money, I could file for divorce, I could cheat on him every night—or not. I hated the fact that he was in danger, hated it every day, but I didn't try to blame fate or God or even the Marine Corps for it (most of the time). This wasn't a cosmic conspiracy or even some grand political agenda. This was just the life we had chosen, and it was too late to change our minds about it now. Maybe that is why it was always so hard for me to answer that constant question from friends and family, "How do you do it?" Maybe I should have responded by asking them, "How do you do your life?" Because really, it all comes down to the simple fact that this is just my life. I did it because the only other choice was to give up, and I wasn't ready to do that.

Did the war change our lives? Absolutely. We all have scars that will follow us for the rest of our days. Our husbands came home changed, and they returned home to wives who had changed as well. There were some marriages that didn't survive the war. Sometimes the stress was just too much, and the gulf that formed between a Marine and his wife was too big to overcome. Most of us in Three-Four made it through the war and the reunion. We hugged our husbands, said our good-byes to our friends, and moved on to new places. Is it over? No, there are some things that never really go away. And those of us still in the Marine Corps know there may always be a next time. That is the sacrifice we make and the service we give. We also serve, those of us who only stand and wait—and pray and cry and hope.

When people ask me about the war and say, "Oh, you must be so proud of your husband," it's easy for me to say yes. I am proud of him and all that he accomplished. I admire him for all his strength and the dedication he has shown not only to the Marine Corps, but to his family as well. I love him, and I would go through another deployment with him just because I love him.

But even more, I am proud to have been a part of the group of women in Three-Four that went through the war together. The strength and courage that those women showed during the worst of times will stay with me forever. I don't know what the deployments would have been like if I hadn't been with Krista and Jennifer and Julie and all the others. What I do know is that they made it easier. Their friendship and support made the good days better and the bad days not quite so horrible. When we didn't have our husbands, we had each other; for that I will always be grateful.

Whatever else happens throughout our life together, Paul and I will always carry the memory of the war with us. It's a part of our marriage now. Some days it is a reminder of all that we have overcome. Other days it's a warning of what may happen again. But when I see my husband in his uniform, standing so straight and tall, I know that in spite of it all, I have made my choice. I am a Marine Corps wife, and I also serve. Am I proud of my husband? More than words can ever say. And I think he's proud of me too.

*Semper Fidelis.*